THE

RIVER AYR
WAY

Other books by Dane Love:

Scottish Kirkyards	Robert Hale	1989
The History of Auchinleck – Village & Parish	Carn Publishing	1991
Pictorial History of Cumnock	Alloway Publishing	1992
Pictorial History of Ayr	Alloway Publishing	1995
Scottish Ghosts	Robert Hale	1995
Scottish Ghosts	Barnes & Noble	1996
Tales of the Clan Chiefs	Robert Hale	1999
The Auld Inns of Scotland	Robert Hale	1997
Guide to Scottish Castles	Lomond Books	1998
Scottish Covenanter Stories	Neil Wilson	2000
Ayr Stories	Fort Publishing	2000
Ayrshire Coast	Fort Publishing	2001
Scottish Spectres	Robert Hale	2001
Scottish Spectres	Ulverston Large Print	2003
Ayrshire: Discovering a County	Fort Publishing	2003
Ayr Past and Present	Sutton Publishing	2003
Lost Ayrshire	Birlinn	2005
Ayr: the Way We Were	Fort Publishing	2006

www.dane-love.co.uk

THE
RIVER AYR
WAY

Dane Love

carn

For Dane Cowan Love and Gillian Hazel Love
— two young companions who enjoyed the walk and stories of places seen.

©Dane Love 2006
First Published in Great Britain 2006

ISBN 0 9518128 4 X
EAN 978 09518128 4 6

Published by
Carn Publishing
Lochnoran House
Auchinleck
Ayrshire
KA18 3JW

Printed by Walker & Connell, Ltd.
Hastings Square
Darvel
Ayrshire
KA17 0DS

Contents

Maps

Illustrations

Introduction

The River Ayr is one of the finest rivers in Scotland, and yet its watercourse is often hidden from public view, meandering through wild moors or snaking through deep gorges. From its source at Glenbuck to the sea at Ayr it passes through some of the wildest countryside in the county, and yet this is the heart of Ayrshire, an area usually associated with mining, Ayrshire cows, and farming. The river has carved for itself a route so difficult of access that man's roadways and communities often turn their back on the course, finding it easier to traverse the countryside by other routes, leaving the river to wildlife.

The River Ayr is 38 miles (63 km) in length, although various measurements of the river give slightly different figures. The basin of the river, or its catchment area, is approximately 222 square miles (574 sq km).

At its start, the Ayr is a moorland stream, flowing from Glenbuck Loch westwards across the moors of Muirkirk and Sorn parishes. The river may be fairly unremarkable here, but it passes through an area rich in history, from industrial heritage at Glenbuck and Muirkirk, to associations with the Covenanters and John Loudon MacAdam. Soon the river begins to carve for itself a glen, as it makes its way through wild countryside towards Sorn, an attractive small village nestling in a hollow formed by the river.

At Catrine, the next village that straddles the river, one can marvel at some of the feats of industrial archaeology, where cotton mills that were as important as New Lanark once existed. Below Catrine the river is crossed by some major bridges, the modern Howford road bridge and the record-holding Ballochmyle railway viaduct, with its massive sandstone arch, springing across the deep gorge.

The minister of Tarbolton, writing in the *New Statistical Account of Scotland* in 1842, noted that the River Ayr:

... is chiefly remarkable, as compared with other rivers of Scotland, for its dark colour, which it derives from two sources – the alluvial matter which is carried along with it, and the dark colour of the strata composing its channels and banks. There has been a very considerable loss of life in the Ayr, owing to the darkness of its waters, concealing from view persons who had ventured into it, deep places, with which the river abounds, termed in the provincial dialect "weels", almost every "weel" bearing the name of some person who has perished in it.

Old mills and weirs exist along the length of the river, and it is crossed by a number of old bridges, such as Sorn, Howford, Stair and Ayr's Auld Bridge. A number of fine old castles and tower houses can be seen, such as Sorn Castle and Stair House, as well as more recent mansions like Auchincruive and Craigie.

Auchincruive has its historical connections with Sir William Wallace, whose ancestors at one time owned the estate, and today it has a number of attractive walks through the policies. There are also connections with Robert Burns, who has associations with numerous places along the riverside, as well as with people whom he knew and conversed with. In his poem, 'The Brigs of Ayr', Burns describes the various sources of the river:

> *When from the hills where springs the brawling Coil,*
> *Or stately Lugar's mossy fountains boil,*
> *Or where the Greenock winds his moorland course,*
> *Or haunted Garpel draws his feeble source,*
> *Arous'd by blustering winds an' spotting thowes,*
> *In monie a torrent down the snaw-broo rowes;*
> *While crashing ice, borne on the roaring speat,*
> *Sweeps dams, an' mills, and brigs, a' to the gate;*
> *And from Glenbuck down to the Ratton-Key,*
> *Auld Ayr is just one lengthen'd tumbling sea.*

Ayr, the county town, is where the river reaches the sea. The River Ayr Walk has been a popular stroll for residents for many years, and it is linked with other routes to create an interesting walk through the centre of town to the south pier of Ayr Harbour, where the river's water looses itself in the Firth of Clyde.

The name Ayr is difficult to explain, though the *Ordnance Gazetteer* states that it come from the Gaelic *a-reidh*, which means 'smooth water'. This was corrupted originally into Are, then Air, and now Ayr. Other possibilities that have been mooted include derivations from *eyri*, which is Old Norse for a gravely bank or thin part of land. Another theory associates the river with the goddess 'Agrona' who was associated with slaughter. On Ptolemy's map of Scotland, which is thought to date from AD 150, the River Vindogara is thought to represent the Ayr, and this may be its original name.

The *Ordnance Gazetteer* also gives a short description of the river, which is worth reproducing:

> Its course, for a few miles, lies through bleak moors and upland meadows; but afterwards traverses a fertile champaign country, chiefly along deep, narrow, bosky dell or chasm. Its principal tributaries are the Garpol [*sic*] the Greenock, the Lugar, and the Coyle. It traverses or bounds the parishes of Muirkirk, Sorn, Auchinleck, Mauchline, Tarbolton, Stair, Ayr and St Quivox, and passes by Muirkirk, Wellwood, Limmerhaugh, Holhouse, Sorn, Catrine, Ballochmyle, Barskimming, Failford, Stair, Auchincruive, and Whitletts; while places near it are Airdsmoss, Auchinleck, Mauchline, Tarbolton, Coylton and St Quivox. Many reaches of it are richly picturesque; many abound with striking close scenes; and not a few are touched graphically, or worked into strong associations, in the poems of Burns.

Many areas of the riverside are renowned for their natural history, none more so than the Ayr Gorge Woodlands of Failford, protected as a wildlife reserve. Here the natural sandstone cliffs have been carved by man to create steps leading to an open pulpit, where the Covenanting minister, Rev Alexander Peden, delivered his last sermon during the years of persecution.

There are a number of Sites of Special Scientific Interest (SSSIs) along the riverside, including Glenbuck Loch, the Muirkirk Uplands, Garpel Water, Greenock Mains, Howford, Failford Gorge and Stairhill. These areas are protected by law for their biological or geological importance.

Much of the countryside around Muirkirk is protected as part of the Muirkirk Uplands Special Protection Area, noted for being breeding grounds for birds such as the hen harrier, red and black grouse, peregrine falcons and merlins.

A number of major floods have occurred on the river over the centuries. Only recent floods are recorded in history, and reference is made to serious damage caused by the raging river in 1877, 1925, 1927 and 1966.

In winter there can be large flows of ice down the river. The still stretches of water freeze up and it is not unknown for the ice to gain a thickness of twenty inches. As the thaw comes the ice is broken and forced downstream, often battering and destroying anything in its path. According to 'Rab the Ramber', writing in 1884, 'the breaking of the ice on the Ayr is one of the grandest and most impressive sights I have ever seen, and must be seen to be appreciated.'

Fishing on the river is controlled by various groups. Management of this is undertaken by the River Ayr Salmon Fishery Board. Approximately twenty per cent of all salmon caught in the county are from the river, averaging around 500 per annum in recent years. The river is also a good source of sea trout.

The Ayrshire Rivers Trust is a charitable organisation that was founded in 2000 to improve the freshwater fish stocks in the county.

As well as being a guidebook to the River Ayr Way, established in 2006 and officially opened on 10 June by Fred Macaulay, this book is also a history and topographical guide to the river itself, and the numerous places of interest that can be found alongside the river, as well as folk associated with the area. I hope that you will enjoy discovering the River Ayr as much as I did.

Dane Love
Auchinleck, June 2006.

1. GLENBUCK to WELLWOOD

The source of the River Ayr is difficult to define, for a number of small streams, or burns as they are known in Scotland, flow from the Glenbuck hills down into the Glenbuck Loch. Of these the Stottencleugh Burn is the larger, and probably has the right to claim to be the infant Ayr. This stream rises on the western slopes of Sclanor Hill, an eminence 1394 feet (425m) above sea level, itself a subsidiary height of the Auchinstilloch and Priesthill hills. Roughly 1260 feet (385m) above sea level a few minor watercourses merge together and the infant Stottencleugh Burn is formed. This drops quickly from the hill, at first heading in a south-casterly direction, as though heading for the Douglas Water, and ultimately the River Clyde, but within a mile and a half it changes course, and keeps its independence, becoming the River Ayr, which flows into the sea at the town of Ayr, around 40 miles from its source.

The Stottencleugh Burn passes through a narrow glen on its way down to Glenbuck, a narrow defile that is afforested to the west. In the glen are the remains of old coal mines, and a few former air shafts can still be made out on the ground. This was part of the Grasshill Mine, which operated in a private capacity as late as 1980.

Soon the remains of the railway viaduct are reached. This was erected in 1883 as part of the Muirkirk & Lesmahagow Junction Railway, one that is legendary hereabouts. When private companies operated the railways there was considerable competition. The Glasgow and South Western Railway Company had its line west of Muirkirk, and the Caledonian Railway Company had a line from Muirkirk eastwards through Douglasdale to link in with the rest of

Lanarkshire. A complicated Act of Parliament was needed to allow either company to expand further, and to prevent the G&SWR from muscling in to the rich coal and iron trade in Lanarkshire. The Caledonian Railway company sought permission to build the railway, and as long as they did so, the G&SWR were unable to extend further eastward. Accordingly a line was laid from near Lesmahagow through Coalburn and across the moors to Muirkirk. Thousands of pounds were spent building it, with three considerable viaducts and various earthworks taking the line across valleys and through the hills. Some say that no train ever ran its length, whereas others claim that there was only ever one, sent along it to test the track and signals. However, the line remained closed, possibly due to the viaduct across the Ayr being unsafe due to mining subsidence. This viaduct, near to Auldhouseburn, was later blown up during the Second World War as practise.

The Stottencleugh Burn flows down past former coal bings and into what was the village of Glenbuck. The village was founded around 1650, but there was no regular employment until 1700 when an English firm starting mining here. This failed and the village declined until the New Mills Weaving Company of Lanark arrived and set up mills in 1760. This again lasted only a short time before the trade was abandoned.

In 1787 English prospectors returned and ironstone and coal was found in sufficient quantity to establish an ironworks. This commenced in 1790 and was in full blast by 1794. As a result the population began to rise.

It was the Glenbuck Ironworks that supplied the Duke of Portland with seventy thousand rails, of three feet in length, which he laid to create a double-track railway from Kilmarnock to Troon. The rails were forty pounds in weight each, and the contract was worth £20,000 in 1808. This railway is thought to be Scotland's first double-tracked line.

At one time Glenbuck had its own quoad sacra parish church, erected in 1881-2 to plans by Robert Ingram at a cost of £2,000. On the front wall of this was a memorial erected by Charles Howatson of Glenbuck in memory of the local Covenanting martyrs. The church was closed in 1954, but stood for many years afterwards. When the church was demolished the Covenanting stone was saved and can now be seen in the kirkyard at Muirkirk.

Glenbuck also had a post office, railway station, public school, savings bank and village hall, but today there is little to hint of a thriving upland community. The site of the village has been virtually destroyed by open cast mining. There are plans to re-establish a community here, perhaps based on crofting principles, with each house having a stretch of land.

Around Glenbuck coal was mined at Airdsgreen, ironstone came from Muirfoot and Bricklow and limestone was quarried at Hareshaw Hill. As each of these sources dried up new mines or quarries were sunk. The population of the village rose to 800 by 1800, and peaked at 1750 in 1900, most of whom were employed in the supply of resources to the works, or in the smelting of iron ore itself.

The ironworks closed in 1813, mainly due to the poor quality of the ironstone available locally. However, the extraction of coal continued, and numerous mines existed all round the village. Some of these were rather small, and today there is virtually nothing to indicate their whereabouts, whereas some of the larger mines have left spoil heaps. In recent years open cast mining has been undertaken on a large scale in the area. The last great opencast, Spireslack, even removed the last remains of the old Glenbuck village.

Glenbuck is still renowned for its former junior football team, known as the Glenbuck Cherrypickers. This team won many titles during its existence, but had to fold in 1932 when most of the residents of the village were rehoused in Muirkirk. The Cherrypickers produced six players who went on to represent Scotland, including Bill Shankly, who was capped thirteen times.

Bill Shankly became a legend in football circles. He was born in 1913, part of a family of five brothers and five sisters. His father, John, was a tailor and also a keen middle distance runner. Bill played initially for the Cherrypickers before moving on to Cronberry Eglinton. He then played for Carlisle United and Preston North End. Bill Shankly's skill as a manager was noted early on, and he managed various clubs before taking over Liverpool Football Club, which he managed between 1959-74. He was renowned for his quotes, in particular that in which he stated, "Some people think football is a matter of life and death, in fact it's more important than that!" Shankly died in 1981. A memorial stone has been erected at Glenbuck to commemorate him, and this can be seen by the side of the road, next to the entrance to Glenbuck Home Farm.

Quoiting was also a popular sport among the miners, and Tom Bone (1871-1920) became both Scottish and British champion – he held the Scottish title for nine years in succession.

Glenbuck Loch was created around 1802 as a storage reservoir for water. Two earthen dams were constructed at either end of the narrow glen to form a loch with a maximum depth of

36 feet. The water was released at six o' clock in the evening, increasing the flow of the River Ayr. This enlarged water flow took twelve hours to make its way downstream to Catrine, where it was used to drive the mill wheels of the cotton works. It was noted that if the river bed was dry, then the water took longer to reach Catrine. At one time there was a second loch, south and west of the A70 road, but this has been drained. The present loch is fairly natural in appearance and is richly wooded other than on the north side, where the steep slopes of Hareshaw Hill rise out of the water. The former line of the Caledonian Railway makes its way through part of the loch, cutting off a small segment.

The River Ayr Way officially starts at a bird-watching hide on the north side of Glenbuck Loch. The hide was erected in 2005 and is located at the water's edge. From viewing slits, walkers can look out over the length of the loch and catch site of various forms of bird life, from swans to herons. Walkers need to make a return route from the hide along paths on the north side of the loch. A couple of hundred yards west of the hide is another wooden building, used by Muirkirk Angling Association. Here are a couple of small wooden jetties for boats. Glenbuck Loch has wild brown trout fishing available by permit, from both bank and boat. Day permits for bank fishing are available from a shop in Muirkirk.

Glenbuck Loch is designated as a Site of Special Scientific Interest (SSSI) due to the fact that fossilised fish can be found in the banks of the loch. The loch is also notable in that ospreys have been spotted in the area.

By the side of the path are a number of small interesting items to look out for. At one point is a stone obelisk, originally a gate post. Also to be seen is a carved totem pole, decorated with wildlife and topped by an eagle's head. The word Muirkirk is carved near the bottom. In the field above the hide one can look at the old trees, still located in their iron protectors, but bursting to get out. A number of old trees can be seen in these former policies, including massive Scots and Douglas pines.

The path continues westwards to the road that once led into Glenbuck House. A parking area for fishermen is located near here. It is apparent that this area was at one time part of an estate's pleasure grounds, for the fences are the typical iron posts and strap, and here and there some of the old iron estate gates can be seen. On some of these the monogram of CH can still be seen, representing Charles Howatson. There are lots of large trees, and the woods are filled with rhododendron bushes and bulbs in the spring.

Two large stone gate piers mark the former entrance to the service area of Glenbuck House. The main drive would have continued straight past these, round to the front of the house, which overlooked the loch. The house was erected in 1879-80 on the site of East Glenbuck farm for the local landowner, Charles Howatson, who had found considerable fame as a breeder of black-faced sheep. The architect was John Murdoch of Ayr. A Scottish baronial styled

Glenbuck Totem Pole

building, the house was demolished in May 1948.

Charles Howatson (1833-1918) was the eldest son of William Howatson of Cronberry (1808-1882). In 1867 his Glenbuck black-faced sheep won at the Royal Highland Show, and one of his rams went on to win the Prince of Wales Gold Medal and Parish Show championships. As a result of money made from farming and other business interests he was able to purchase Daldorch House near Catrine, where he lived prior to building Glenbuck House. By 1900 he owned a considerable upland estate, covering much of the upper Glenmuir and around Glenbuck. He was buried in Auchinleck kirkyard.

From the old gate piers the Way follows the drive downhill to the cottage near to the entrance gates. To the right, on an elevated hillside location, stands Glenbuck Home Farm, a courtyard steading that was contemporary with Glenbuck House. Sporting the traditional Scots corbie-stepped gables, the courtyard is reached through an arched pend, over which is carved CH in a monogram and the date 1879. Above this are six small doocot entrances. Behind the steading, on the Hareshaw Burn, is a small waterfall.

The Stottencleugh Burn is crossed beyond the gatehouse cottage by a low bridge, with white-painted cast iron parapets. Just beyond this, to the right, is the memorial to Bill Shankly. The Way follows the public road southwards from here, through a narrow glen that is adorned by tall trees and rhododendrons. An old kissing gate gives access to West Glenbuck farm.

Near to where the minor road meets the A70, one can look to the left and see the old sluices at the north end of the dam that created Glenbuck Loch. The River Ayr proper starts here, and one can stand at the head of the sluice and see the infant river flowing down to a little bridge under the A70.

The A70 is followed westwards by the River Ayr Way for 450 yards to a gate leading off the road to the south. This is located opposite an old kissing gate that once gave access to Newmains Cottage, long-since abandoned and converted for agricultural use. As the path makes its way westwards, it passes an old milestone which, at the time of writing, was lying on its side, indicating that Douglas is six miles to the east and that Edinburgh is 46 miles away. Soon the former Catcraig Quarry is seen, a small quarry on the north side of the road. It is here that the Way makes its way onto the former Douglasdale branch of the Caledonian railway line, and begins to follow it westwards for three and a half miles. Where the path joins the line can be seen the brick foundations of an old railway building, and immediately west of this is seen the remains of the platform of Glenbuck Station, the sides of which were supported by upended railway sleepers.

The railway was originally opened for goods traffic on 1 January 1873 and for passenger traffic on 1 June 1874. The line was created by the Caledonian Railway Company to link its network in Lanarkshire, from Lanark to Muirkirk, where it joined the Glasgow and South Western Railway Company's lines. When this missing link was built there was now a direct rail link from Ayr to Edinburgh, but on the first day that the service was offered in June 1878 the first two trains to leave ran without any passengers. Indeed, the first six trains ran with less than half a dozen passengers in total. For passengers wishing to make their way from Ayr to Edinburgh it was in fact quicker and no more expensive to journey via Glasgow. The line was soon closed to through passenger traffic, but it held its own with freight, coal and ironstone being transported between pits and ironworks in

Lanarkshire and Ayrshire.

From Glenbuck Station to Douglas West Station was six miles by train, but near to Monksfoot was Inches Station, which led many an old wag to announce that 'There's only Inches between Glenbuck and Douglas'.

The former railway line makes for level and straight walking, where one can get a pace on and cover ground in a relatively quick time. To the south are the hills of Belt Knowe, Brack Hill, Little Cairn Table and Cairn Table, forming an ever increasing series of heights marking the boundary between Ayrshire and Lanarkshire. The name of one of the heights, Ettrick Cairn, which lies to the south of Brack Hill, recalls the fact that at one time this was the western extremity of the massive Ettrick Forest, a mediaeval hunting ground.

At first the infant Ayr winds is way across the moor to the south of the railway, below Little Darnhunch and Darnhunch. Most of the watercourse is hidden from view by scrubby woodland. Much of this low-lying ground, north of Darnhunch, was at one time a second Glenbuck Reservoir, known as the Lower Reservoir. The remains of the earthen dam can still be seen, making its way across the valley and breached by a large hole through which the Ayr now flows. The lower loch was probably contemporary with the existing Glenbuck Loch, but it was drained when the railway was laid through the valley.

The River Ayr crosses the railway to the north at the same point as the track accessing Darnhunch farm passes under the railway, or at least did, for the arch of the bridge has been removed. The Ayr then flows on the northern side of the railway, gradually gathering strength as it takes in lesser burns and streams to make it into a larger watercourse. It is really only after the river subsumes the West Burn from the south and the Ponesk Burn from the north that it forms a sizeable watercourse, one that is difficult to cross dry-shod.

To the north of the former railway line the low hillsides opposite have been subject to opencast coal mining, the former Airdsgreen mine having bitten into the low hills as far back as Glenbuck and west towards Lightshaw. There are still parts of the mine remaining. To the west, on the former Lightshaw opencast site, can be seen two modern standing stones, erected to mark the site of the mine and as a point of interest on the hillside.

Lower down the slopes, in a field by the side of the A70 at Lightshaw, can be seen a real standing stone of some antiquity. Little is known about this ancient stone, other than at one time it was supposed to have a circle of lesser stones around it. There are also claims that at one time there were carvings on the stone, but these have long-since been erased by the cattle which use the stone for rubbing.

On the south side of the old railway can be seen former quarries and other works, though in most cases these were on a small scale and have now grown over with grass and shrubs. The bridge over the West Burn survives, its stone arch still carrying the footpath. On the parapets, which have lost their top layer of stone, can be seen numbers and letters carved by the masons to identify the stones. On the south side of the bridge, much of the underbuilding has been either washed away or robbed. Shortly to the west the path passes through a kissing gate at the march fence between Darnhunch and Crossflatt farms. To the north a tiny footbridge, built for use by sheep, could be used to allow the River Ayr to be crossed in order to reach the A70.

Across the River Ayr from the footpath can be seen the line of an early railway that made its way from Crossflatt to the old bridge that was north of Ashawburn. It continued at one time north of the A70 (lost due to opencast mining) right into the village of Glenbuck.

Soon the former cottage of Ashawburn is reached, now a ruin on the southern side of the railway. At one time a track led from here north towards the A70, crossing the Ayr by a footbridge, but the bridge no longer exists (though still shown on some modern maps), and the track is virtually invisible on the ground. The deck of the railway bridge across the track to Ashawburn has been removed, leaving only the stone abutments.

Ashawburn cottage is visible south of the sheep pens. Built of brick (made by 'McDonald Braidwood') and covered with rough cast, the cottage has some sandstone lintels, and the old fireplace can still be seen inside. The cottage had at some point been adapted by the farmer for storage, a large doorway having been created on the north wall, but it has now been totally abandoned.

South of Ashawburn is an extensive area that has been quarried for limestone. In fact, the original Ashawburn cottage was removed when quarrying took place where it stood. It was located further south. Even the Ashaw Burn was re-routed, the upper reaches of it being diverted into the stream to the east. The knolls and gullies of the limestone quarries have almost all grown over, and today the Ashaw Glen has a number of old Scots Pines growing within it.

To the north, at the foot of the Ashaw Burn, stands another old ruin, though little more than the corner stones of the walls can be seen. This was the Walkmill, originally two storeys in height, and where flax was dressed. The building was last occupied in 1926.

If one looks to the north of Ashawburn, just upstream from the Walkmill, one can make out the old dam across the Ayr that marked the start of the Muirkirk Canal. Water followed a level channel west from here, terminating at the Ironworks. The waterway was created in 1790 and was four feet deep. It was sixteen feet wide at the top and the sides tapered to the bottom, which was four feet wide. Before the construction of the railway that the River Ayr Way follows, the canal made its way along this direction, and much of it can still be made out on the ground. At one time there were suggestions made that the canal could be continued to Ayr, but these were never pursued. Today there are no open stretches of water, but the line it took is apparent and marshy.

Five hundred yards west of Ashawburn are a number of former railway junctions. A branch strikes to the south, linking with another line that ran north/south, passing under the main line. These branches were used to transport limestone from the old mines and quarries that existed to the south, adjacent to the large sheep shed that can be seen. The original deck of the bridge here, and of another to the west, have gone, but the granite blocks inserted into the sandstone piers can still be seen. These were harder stones that could better withstand the force applied by the railway.

Looking north, one can see Lightshaw farm, with its standing stone, and on the hillside higher up the earthworks of old pits and quarries. The line of the old railway can be seen crossing the glen, the viaduct virtually gone. Only a few pillars and buttresses remain, the rest blown up.

On the low-lying ground on the north side of the River Ayr, at the foot of the Haw Burn, can be seen a number of large boulders, arranged like a simple version of the Stones of Calanais, or some similar prehistoric stone circle. This one is nowhere so old, for they were erected in 2000 as the Millennium Stones. A track to the stones can be followed from the A70 near Torhill Cottages to the north.

The two and a half storey Kerlstone House is visible on the north side of the river. This was the old manse of Muirkirk and it was erected in 1801 at a cost of £456. The builder was a Muirkirk wright, Alexander Stewart. The parish church is visible in the village beyond, a light coloured church building that is castellated in style. Behind it, higher up, is the red sandstone Roman Catholic chapel of St Thomas.

The old line is followed westwards towards Crossflatt farm, which lies on the southern side of the railway, within trees. The farmhouse is two and a half storeys in height, and is rendered white. Crossflatt was used as a place of hiding during the time of the Covenanters, when Presbyterian Scots were hunted and persecuted by the Episcopalian soldiers of King Charles I and II. From 1638 until 1689 the 'fifty years struggle' saw many men hunted down and either tortured and killed, or else dragged off for execution in Edinburgh. All over Ayrshire the Covenanters were strong, and we will come upon many other places associated with them on the journey down the River Ayr. The path veers off of the railway bed to the north, arriving at an old railway bridge across the farm road. The path descends to the road, which can be followed north across the River Ayr by the Crossflatt Bridge and to the A70 at the east end of Muirkirk if desired.

South of Crossflatt is Auldhouseburn farm. Part of the farmhouse is of a considerable age, and local tradition claims that Mary Queen of Scots visited this farm at one time. When this was is unknown, and she definitely did not visit during her tour of Ayrshire in 1563. However, on her flight from the Battle of Langside, where her supporters were defeated on 13 May 1568, Mary may have come this way, keeping to remote locations where she knew there were followers of her cause.

Auldhouseburn was also used by Covenanters in the seventeenth century as a place of hiding, and local tradition claims that there is a tunnel from the house out to the moors. This may have been used by the occupant of the house at that time, known Covenanter, John Campbell. Part of the house dates from 1610 but it was rebuilt in 1884. The farm, which is often pronounced 'Allersburn', is not really visible from the footpath.

From the old bridge at Crossflatt, the River Ayr Way follows the road north-westwards, then turns left, onto the road to Auldhouseburn, basically missing the bungalow that has been built between the two roads. On the south side of the road are the remains of an old pit, one of many in the district. This was officially Auldhouseburn Colliery, but it was better known to locals as Bankhead Pit. Here, on 11 March 1898, there was an inrush of water which killed three men. But for the bravery of others, the death toll would have been much higher.

The Way leaves the railway for one thousand yards beyond Auldhouseburn road. A kissing gate gives access to an old track. To the north are the remains of the Bankhead cottages, a row of miners' houses. The pairs of stones at either side of the fireplace stick through the turf that has virtually engulfed the remains of the foundations. The houses have long been in ruins, for a sizeable tree grows within what would have been one of them.

From Bankhead the Way makes its way around a former bing, from where views across the River Ayr to Muirkirk can be seen. It actually follows the embankment on the north side of the Muirkirk Canal, the boggy line of which is obvious alongside. In front, to the west, the tower of Kames Institute can be seen, its spires pointing heavenward. A small bridge across the Auldhouse Burn brings the walker back onto the old railway. The burn drops through an attractively wooded glen, and a small waterfall can be heard at times. The path makes its way along the south side of the canal for a stretch, before the waterway peters out, having been filled in with waste. At this point the canal actually fed a sizeable reservoir, adjacent to the Muirkirk Ironworks, and water from it was able to flow down to a second reservoir, also long filled in.

The route follows the old railway line, before heading further south. The woodland to the south was planted in 2005. The path arrives at an old track that links Kames with Auldhouseburn, next to a gate from the wood out into the open moor. From this point views east can be seen to Little Cairn Table. The track is followed westwards alongside a haulage contractor's yard, with red bungalow, occupying the site of Muirkirk Station and before that limekilns associated with the ironworks. A high sandstone wall separates the path from the Furnace Road below. The path reaches the public road at Kames, next to the walkers' car park.

The car park is often used as the starting point for the strenuous walk up to the summit of Cairn Table, the prominent hill to the south. Located on the border between Ayrshire and Lanarkshire, Cairn Table rises 1945 feet (593m) above sea level. On its summit are two Bronze Age burial cairns, but the tall cairn visible on the skyline is a war memorial, erected in 1920 by the locals.

Kames was at one time almost as populous as Muirkirk and had numerous rows of miners' cottages closely packed together on a site now occupied by the race track. Here were around ten rows, home to 1064 residents in 1913. Compared with other Ayrshire miners' rows, the houses at Kames were reasonably good, and many residents rented more than one to give them more space. However, the houses became too outdated for modern living, and from 1930 onwards a programme of re-housing commenced, though this was interrupted by the war. Eventually, by 1960 most of the rows had been cleared, and the population moved to the Smallburn estate at the west end of Muirkirk. Today only a few buildings survive. Today the site of the rows is home to

Muirkirk Golf Club, founded in 1991, which has a nine-hole par 34 course. Day tickets are available. On part of the old railway and sidings, as well as where many miners' rows stood, is a car race track, operated by East Ayrshire Car Club, where various types of races are held throughout the season.

To the north of the old railway line, between it and the River Ayr, stood Muirkirk Ironworks. These were established in 1786 when coal, limestone and ironstone were discovered in reasonable quantity on the lands hereabouts. By 1796 three blast-furnaces had been erected by the Muirkirk Iron Company. The business struggled for a time before being taken over by the larger Eglinton Iron Company in 1856. The furnaces produced iron for many years, before finally closing in 1923.

At one time there was a large colliery at Kames, sunk in 1870. The first shaft was around 600 feet deep. A disaster took place there on Tuesday 19 November 1957 when gas exploded underground, killing seventeen miners. The pit at Kames later reopened, and was the last working mine at Muirkirk until it was closed in June 1968.

Prominent at the centre of Kames is the former Ironworks Institute, its tall clock tower visible from afar in the vicinity. The building was erected in 1904 as a community resource for the miners. It had a billiard room, library and reading room, function

Kames Institute

hall, games room and ancillary facilities. The institute was later closed, and for a number of years the building was used as an outdoor activity centre.

Immediately to the south-west of the institute stood Kames Parish Church, known locally for its attractive interior. This church was erected in 1903-4 to plans by Robert Ingram, but it was closed in 1952. Following a disastrous fire in Muirkirk Parish Church in 1949, the pews and a stained glass window were removed from Kames Church and installed in Muirkirk Parish Church when it was restored.

The Way makes its way behind the institute and back onto what the locals know as the Old Sanquhar Road. This detour to the rear of the institute takes one round what was known as Linkyburn Square, where there were miners' houses at one time. To the south, and still to be made out on the ground, is the former football field of Muirkirk Juniors, abandoned when the new Burnside Park was opened in Muirkirk. The old pitch was known as Ladeside Park and at first it was formed of blaes, or remains from the ironworks, but it was latterly turfed.

The Old Sanquhar Road was constructed in 1790 as part of the Glasgow to Dumfries road. Most of the route between Glasgow and Dumfries is still used today, but the stretch south of Muirkirk as far as Fingland (an isolated farm six miles north of Sanquhar) was quickly abandoned for its remoteness, and today stretches of the road can no longer be made out on the ground, especially south of the Wardlaw pass.

The Old Sanquhar Road is followed from Kames south towards Springhill cottage, home of the gamekeeper on this part of Dumfries House grouse moors. The cottage is an old yellow sandstone building and was originally known as Midhouse of Kaimes, replacing an earlier building of the same name, further north.

On the opposite side of the track from the cottage, and slightly to the south, can be seen the ruins of Springhill House, located within trees. This was the oldest of the manager's houses in the district, built around 1786 for the manager of the British Tar Works. The first occupant of the house was Alexander Cochrane and later it was the home of John Loudon MacAdam, of road-making fame.

John Loudon MacAdam (1756-1836) was born in Ayr, in an ancient house now known as Lady Cathcart's House, which still stands in the Sandgate. The house dates from the seventeenth century, but in 1991 it was restored by the Scottish Historic Buildings Trust and the ground floor is now occupied by the local tourist information centre. MacAdam was the son of James MacAdam and Susanna Cochrane, niece of the 7th Earl of Dundonald. MacAdam came to Muirkirk in 1790 to work as manager of the 9th Earl of Dundonald's (1749-1831) tar works. The works operated from 1786, and produced tar (used mainly on ships' hulls), coke, lampblack, and varnish. MacAdam borrowed £14,000 to purchase the

John Loudon MacAdam

business in 1790, but he quarrelled with the Muirkirk Iron Company over the supply of coke, and this dragged on until 1803. The business supplied MacAdam with an income from then on, and for a time was managed by his son, William MacAdam. The works have long gone, being closed in 1827, but the site of them is marked by a stone-built cairn, located by the side of the Old Sanquhar Road, five hundred yards south of Springhill House, and just off the Way. The cairn is readily visible from the road, and was erected in 1931. It has a slab bearing the inscription:

> *In memory of John Loudoun MacAdam, the famous road-maker 1756-1836. This cairn marks the site of his tar kilns, 1786-1827, and is built with stones from them in 1931.*

Just to the south of Springhill the Way turns westwards, following an old track towards Tibbie's Brig. By the side of the track are old sheep pens, mainly formed by upended railway sleepers. At the end of the stone dike is a steel stile, allowing walkers to head north along the path through the golf course, past Kames farm and back to the A70 at Smallburn. Walkers should take care of flying golf balls!

On either side of the track at this point can be seen the grassy mounds marking the outline of walls that formed Coltburn. This was a small community formed of rows of houses facing each other across the track. These miners' houses must have been some of the oldest in the district, for the Ordnance Survey map of 1860 depicts them as ruinous. A local poet, Hugh Park, wrote verses on 'The Auld Coutburn Raw':

Come listen noo, people, till my story I tell,
It's on some auld hooses – it's lang since they fell –
On the lands o' Kaimeshill, on the road tae the 'Shaw,
And the name they go under is the Auld Coutburn Raw.

Hugh Park concludes the poem by indicating that his father, who had died aged 62, was a tenant in the row.

The track continues westwards, passing an old mine shaft to the south, one of many that litter the moors hereabouts. To the north can be seen more mounds indicating former buildings, one of which was known as Cochrane Lodge. The name Cochrane is obviously associated with the Earl of Dundonald, being the family name. Near to it is a steel picnic table, erected in memory of David Docherty (1927-2002), who was involved in restoring Tibbie's Brig, visible below. Also visible to the south, at the mouth of a small stream, are some earthworks associated with an old limekiln and lime works that once existed here.

Tibbie's Brig is how the locals refer to what was originally known as Garpel Bridge. Tibbie (or Isobel) Pagan (1741-1821), was a poetess whose work was known to Robert Burns. She was born in New Cumnock parish but moved to Muirkirk in 1755 and then to Garpelside in 1785, where she established a small inn near to the bridge (which had still to be erected), supplying ale to local miners and ironstone workers. Her house here was supposed to have been erected by Admiral Keith Stewart using remains of an old brick kiln that was part of the tar works. Pagan had a squint and was lame, but her character endeared her to many. Little of her poetry is known today, but she wrote the original version of 'Ca' the Yowes tae the Knowes', that Burns adapted and rewrote. A small volume of her poetry, entitled *Songs and Poems on Several Occasions* was published in 1803, but copies of this are extremely rare. She was buried in the old churchyard of Muirkirk, where her headstone can still be seen.

While waters wimple tae the sea,
While day blinks in the life sae hie,
Till clay cauld death shall blin' my e'e,
Ye shall be my dearie.

Ca' the yowes tae the knowes,
Ca' them whaur the heather grows,
Ca' them whaur the burnie rows,
My bonie dearie.

Tibbie's Brig was erected in 1793 to serve the numerous mine workings and industries that littered this moor at one time. It gradually fell into ruin, but in 1995 it was restored to its former glory by local volunteers and inmates from Dungavel Prison. A plaque on the parapet commemorates another of those responsible for rebuilding it. It was reopened on 27 August 1995.

On the south side of the bridge is a memorial to Tibbie Pagan, erected in 1931, complete with representations of the ewes that she referred to in her song. It bears a small plaque stating:

Tibbie Pagan (poetess). 'Ca' the yowes tae the knowes' 1741-1820.

From Tibbie's Brig the Way follows an old track southwards up the slope before heading westwards. By the side of a small stream are large blocks of fragmented concrete, part of old coal mines. To the south can be seen the remains of more old miners' cottages. The track joins another from the south, which follows the line of an old railway that was used to transport coal to the ironworks. The track is now mainly used to access the grouse moors to the south. From the junction the track is followed north to the former railway bridge. To the north was an old cottage named Bluelour.

The Way passes under the track of a dismantled railway, a continuation of the one followed

Garpel Bridge

westwards from Glenbuck. This railway was opened on 9 August 1848, a branch from the line at Auchinleck to Muirkirk being created to allow coal and ironstone, as well as passengers, to access the flourishing community of Muirkirk. The line operated until 1964 for passengers, though it remained open for a further four years for the transportation of coal before it was fully closed. However the path keeps to the track heading north westwards to the Tilework Plantation and another railway line, which is followed westward for about half a mile towards Upper Wellwood farm.

To the south rises the prominent hill of Wardlaw, reaching 1631 feet (497m) in height. The summit has the remains of a few Bronze Age burial cairns, but these have been denuded of their loose stone to allow the erection of a memorial cairn to John George Alexander Baird (1854-1917), a local landowner and MP (1886-1906). Baird was a partner in the local iron and coal works, a nephew of the more famous James Baird of Gartsherrie (1802-76) who was one of Scotland's richest men in his day. J. G. A. Baird gifted a few public buildings to Muirkirk and wrote a small history of the village entitled *Muirkirk in Bygone Days*, published in 1910. Baird lived at Wellwood House, an ancient residence that was extended by him in 1878 into a fine baronial mansion.

The old railway track is followed past some woods to the side of Upper Wellwood farm. This farm has a sizeable blonde sandstone farmhouse, two storeys in height and having large Georgian windows. The gables have crow-steps, and there are some older cottages around the steading. A number of old date stones are incorporated into the building, one a marriage stone of 1606.

The Way continues west along the old railway line, which is newer than the 1848 line, through part of the Peathill Plantation. Just after the Way crosses the

Willaim Adam's grave

Proscribe Burn the path strikes north, through an old stand of pines. Down to the right, by the burn side, a martyr's grave can be seen. This small headstone within iron railings marks the grave of William Adam, a servant at the farm, who was shot here by Captain Dalzeal in March 1685. He was awaiting his loved one when the soldiers out searching for Covenanters found him and began to question him. His answers were not to their liking, and he had a Bible on his possession, so they shot him and he was buried on the spot. It has been speculated that Adam may have been shot in error for another. During the time of the Covenanters Upper Wellwood was home to William Campbell, and his sons William and John. The sons suffered imprisonment and all had to live rough on the moors for a time, but all survived until after the revolution.

The Way follows the west side of the Proscribe Burn north to the side of the River Ayr once more, having left it about three miles earlier. The path passes through a wood planted in 2005 and reaches the riverside. The River Ayr has made its way alongside the edge of Muirkirk in the meantime. From near the foot of the burn a view can be made eastwards to the houses of Smallburn at the west end of Muirkirk.

The path follows the bank of the river westwards towards Greenside Plantation. On the north bank of the river is the site of Wellwood House. When the house was first built is unknown, but reference to a house here, perhaps an old tower house or castle, dates from the sixteenth century. The house was owned at that time by the Campbell family, perhaps scions of the Campbells of Loudoun Castle, who owned extensive estates in the eastern part of Ayrshire. The last Campbell of Wellwood, physician John, lost funds in the Ayr Bank crash and sold the estate to Admiral Keith Stewart in 1785. Later owners were Lord G. C. Bentinck and then the Baird family. Extensions were added in 1740 and 1878. Wellwood House was demolished in 1928.

Wellwood House had a reputation for being haunted by a ghost named Beenie, the spirit of a female who is supposed to have been murdered in the house. She has been seen in the woods around the house, but most often within, on a stairway. One of the treads had what appeared to be blood stains on it, but despite regular scrubbings, always reappeared. At length the owners asked a local mason to insert a new tread, but he is supposed to have died within a few hours of completing the job.

An old steel girder footbridge crosses the River Ayr from the Greenside Plantation to the site of Wellwood House. This is marked by a pile of masonry rubble, some of the shaped stones being visible, such as window openings and fireplace lintels. The old farm of Middle Wellwood formerly stood adjacent to the house, but at the 1878 rebuilding a new farm was erected in the Haystackhill Plantation to the north, leaving the country house standing alone in its policies. The fact that this was at one time someone's pleasure grounds is only really apparent by the group of rhododendron bushes growing along the steep riverside bank in the Greenside Plantation.

The south side of the River Ayr is followed westward for one mile from Wellwood to Wellwood Bridge. Hereabouts the river is deep and flows sedately through open farmland. The water is a dark peaty colour. The path is followed around a large meander. On the north side of the river the remains of a Bronze Age burial cairn can be found in a small wood, and another low hill thereabouts is known as Beacon Hill, indicative of a former use. At the north west corner of the meander is the Marchouse plantation, comprising Scots Pines. Various stands of these majestic trees can be seen on the south side of the river. The path makes its way along the southern bank of the river towards the Wellwood Bridge. Just short of the main road are two steel uprights, on either side of the river, with pulleys.

Wellwood Bridge is crossed by the A70. The concrete bridge was erected in 1931 to replace an earlier bridge, which was in fact named Muirmill Bridge. The Way does not join the A70 at the bridge – instead it makes its way alongside the southern edge of a pine wood. It meets a track that heads south to Wellwood Siding Cottage, visible in ruins to the south. Here also a view can be seen across the moors to Wardlaw Hill (with its cairn) and Cairn Table. The rounded green knolls are in fact remnants of old pit bings, long overgrown. The track is followed north back to the A70, near to the electricity sub-station.

The A70 is crossed to the opposite side, and the path then makes its way westward through a pine wood for 600 yards to Laigh Wellwood Bridge, where a minor road crosses the River Ayr. Between the two Wellwood bridges the village of Wellwood Row once stood, rows of miners' houses facing each other across the road. There were five rows of houses at one time, three of them on the north side of the road, and two on the south. The Six Inch Ordnance Survey map of 1860 shows a small building of some sort in the centre of the road, perhaps a toll house. A toll cottage was established here in 1789, relocating one from Muirkirk to this spot. Unlike many other old miners' rows hereabouts, the site of the houses can no longer be made out on the ground, and tall pine trees occupy the space. In the middle of what was the village is a milestone, indicating Cumnock is seven miles distant, and Ayr 23 miles, whereas Muirkirk is three miles back to the east.

The Way has bypassed Muirkirk to the south of the village, but the river keeps much closer to the upland village. The east end of the village is the oldest part, where at one time the village of Garan, or Garron, stood. In 1631 the 'Moor Kirk of Kyle' was established, and 30,282 acres of Mauchline parish were disjoined to become Muirkirk parish. The present parish church is a fairly unique building, erected in 1812-14 to plans of William Stark. Erected at a cost of £1876, the church is a rather low-hung building, even its castellated tower being rather squat. It has a window by Stephen Adam, taken from Kames Church.

Around the kirk is an old graveyard, with the site of the earlier church behind. In the kirkyard are graves to John Smith, a Covenanter who was shot by Colonel Buchan and Lockhart of the Lee in February 1685, Tibbie Pagan, a poetess, John Lapraik, poet, and many old gravestones. Here also can be seen a large boulder commemorating the Covenanters of the district, formerly located on Glenbuck Church. A plaque on the church wall commemorates J. G. A. Baird of Wellwood.

Slightly higher up is the Roman Catholic chapel of St Thomas the Apostle, erected in 1906. Uniquely, much of the material used to build the chapel was brought to Muirkirk from Belgium. St Thomas's church is open by arrangement through Scotland's

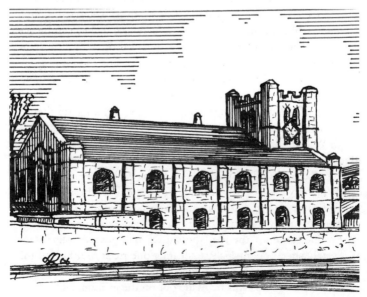

Muirkirk Parish Church

Churches Scheme. The older chapel is located lower down the Kirkgreen, on the west side, now used as a church hall.

The main centre of Muirkirk is now located further west, at the junction of Glasgow Road with Main Street. Here are a number of old traditional buildings, complete with a selection of shops, inns, post office and other services. There is a caravan park by the side of the River Ayr, accessed from Furnace Road.

At the junction of Muirkirk Road and Main Street is a memorial garden, complete with a statue of a miner, sculpted by Kirti Mandir, and unveiled on 21 June 2004 by Jack McConnell MSP in memory of the 79 local mineworkers who lost their lives in the winning of coal 1892-1966. Here also can be seen the Victoria Jubilee memorial that was transported here from Glenbuck, as well as the Church of Scotland symbol rescued when Glenbuck Church was demolished. Around the garden are information boards detailing the history of the parish.

At the west end of the village, opposite the housing scheme of Smallburn, is a lay-by with a number of memorials, as well as a tall wooden totem pole, erected in 2006. A cairn commemorates the local Covenanters, and other structures, including a small bridge, recollect other aspects from Muirkirk's history. Another memorial, in the form of a tall obelisk, in memory of the local Covenanters can be seen in the new cemetery, located on Glasgow Road. It was erected in 1887 by Charles Howatson of Glenbuck in Queen Victoria's Jubilee year.

Muirkirk has a population of around 1,630, but this has fallen considerably from a high of 5,670 in 1901. Muirkirk grew with the formation of ironworks in 1787, and the ongoing mining for coal, but today there is little immediate employment, and most residents have to travel for work.

2. Wellwood to Catrine

To the west of Muirkirk, at Nether Wellwood, the Way crosses the concrete Laigh Wellwood Bridge and immediately strikes west alongside the northern bank of the river. The path follows the edge of the holm, with views south to Nether Wellwood farm. The older farm house can be seen to the rear of the present large dwelling. The poet, James Hyslop (1798-1827), who wrote the popular verse, 'A Cameronian Dream', which refers to the killing of the Covenanter, Rev Richard Cameron, came to work here as a shepherd in 1812. Hyslop was born at Damhead Cottage, at Kirkland farm, near Crawick in Dumfriesshire, where a stone obelisk commemorates him. He wrote articles for the *Edinburgh Magazine*, whose editor, Lord Jeffrey, encouraged him. In 1827 Hyslop began work as a tutor on board long-haul ships. He died of fever on one of these voyages off the Cape Verde islands and was buried at sea. A collection of poems by Hyslop was published in 1887 and in 1889 'A Cameronian Dream' was made into a cantata by Hamish MacCunn.

Near the end of the holm are old stepping stones, and a bridge giving access to the west side of the river. Near here is the site of Muir Mill, or Muirsmill. This was the parish mill of Muirkirk, and all farms were thirled to it, meaning that, as part of their rental agreement, they had to use the services of this mill for grinding corn. It had a breast paddle wheel when it was in operation, and this drove one pair of stones. The mill seems to have disappeared by the time of the 1860 survey. It was here that the poet Tibbie Pagan lived when she first came to Muirkirk, and later another poet, John Lapraik, when he had to sell his property.

On the south side of the River Ayr is the extensive raised bog known as Airds Moss. Since 2004 around 720 acres of this has been protected by the RSPB. The reserve is mainly for the protection of hen harriers, peregrine falcons, merlins and grouse, though more common birds such as peewits and oyster catchers can be seen. The reserve is also home to cuckoos, crossbills and skylarks, the raised bog being ideal territory for them. The Way passes through the reserve as far as the bridge across the River Ayr south of Greenock Mains.

On the moor is a memorial marking the spot where the Battle of Airds Moss took place on 20 July 1680, between Rev Richard Cameron and his followers and around 120 well-equipped government soldiers under Sir Andrew Bruce of Earlshall. Cameron decided to fight, but before taking up arms said a short prayer, in which he included the immortal lines, 'Lord, spare the green and take the ripe.' The battle was bloody, neither side taking quarter. Cameron was struck down, as were eight other Covenanters. These were Michael Cameron, Robert Dick, Captain John Fuller (or Fowler), John Gemmel, James Gray of Chryston, John Hamilton, Robert Paterson of Kirkhill in Cambusnethan parish, and Thomas Watson. The head and hands of Richard Cameron were cut off by Robert Murray and taken to Edinburgh to claim the bounty. He handed them over to the Privy Council declaring, 'These are the head and hands of a man who lived praying and preaching, and died praying and fighting.' The nine Covenanters' bodies were buried on the moss, where two memorials mark their graves. The soldiers' loss was 28 dead. Bruce was given £500 for his victory and Sir John Cochrane of Ochiltree, who had directed him to where Cameron and his men were, was awarded 10,000 merks.

The pathway is followed alongside the river towards Upper Tarrioch Holm. In a large meander on the north side of the river can be seen a pointed cairn. This is a memorial to John Lapraik (1727-1807), a minor poet, who lived on a farm that stood here at one time, named Laigh Dalfram. In his day the name would have been spelled 'Dalquhram'. Lapraik was acquainted with Robert Burns, and wrote to him in verse, eliciting three rhyming responses from the bard in 1785 in his 'Epistles to John Lapraik':

> *But Mauchline Race or Mauchline Fair,*
> *I should be proud to meet you there:*
> *We'se gi'e ae night's discharge to care,*
> *If we forgather;*
> *And ha'e a swap o' rhymin'-ware*
> *Wi' ane anither.*

John Lapraik's Cairn

John Lapraik lost financially with the collapse of the Ayr bank of Douglas, Heron & Company in 1772, and was forced out of his farm. He moved to Muirsmill and then to Netherwood farm, which is located on the banks of the Greenock Water, just over a mile to the north-east of Laigh Dalfram. He returned to Muirsmill (where Burns is known to have spent at least one night) then moved to Nether Wellwood farm, which was passed on the Way one mile earlier. Lapraik then moved into Muirkirk and ran a post office and alehouse at the Kirkgreen for a time. He was jailed in Ayr in 1785 for his debts but in 1788 was able to have his poems published in Kilmarnock. He was buried in the old kirkyard in Muirkirk, where his grave can still be found. The memorial cairn was unveiled on 17 July 1914 by the Lapraik Burns Club of Muirkirk. Within the cairn were preserved a number of local mementoes, as well as a piece of wood taken from the Auld Bridge in Ayr.

John Lapraik wrote a song entitled 'When I Upon Your Bosom Lean', which was included in Johnson's Musical Museum.

35

This is supposed to have been composed whilst locked up in the gaol at Ayr, a result of his financial debts. Burns presented a copy of this book to Captain Riddell of Glenriddell and in a footnote to the song wrote 'this song was the work of a very worthy, facetious old fellow, John Lapraik, of Dalfram, near Muirkirk. He has often told me that he composed this song one day when his wife had been fretting over their misfortunes.'

> *When I upon your bosom lean,*
> *Enraptured I do call thee mine,*
> *I glory in those sacred ties,*
> *That made us ane wha ance were twain.*

On the adjoining meander, but on the south side of the river, can be seen the remains of a very early ironworks. Maps name this as the Old Foundry Holm, but it was referred to as the 'Spadeworks' in old accounts. The path makes its way alongside the old lade that directed water to the forge, the embankments easily seen to the north side. At the west end of the dried lade can be seen a wide hollow that had been a reservoir for water, with the remains of the dam. There are also a few fragments of stone buildings, including an archway.

The Tarrioch Ironworks were established around 1730 by the Earl of Cathcart. Haematite, with an iron content of up to 80%, was mined on the Pennel Burn, on the slopes of Auchenlongford Hill to the north west. This had to be transported on pack-horse to Ayr, then by boat to Argyll where it was smelted at the Bunawe Ironworks by the Lorn Furnace Company. The ingots of pig iron were then returned to Tarrioch for further working.

The iron works were operated mainly by Englishmen, who lived in a row of houses on the north side of the Muirkirk-Sorn road, between Townhead of Greenock and Townfoot, which used to be quarter of a mile to the west of Townhead. The heat for the forge was supplied by burning wood and peat, but the former ran out quickly and the latter was in too slow a supply due to the time it took to dry out. As a result the works did not last very long.

The Way continues on the south side of the River Ayr past the small mound known as the Witch Knowe to Nether Tarrioch Holm. On the hillside to the south the ruins of a stone gable can be seen. This was Nether Tarrioch farm.

The river is then crossed onto the lands of Greenock Mains farm, and a path between two fences is followed towards the B743. Greenock Mains was the home of Covenanter Thomas Richard, who was taken from his home by soldiers and dragged to

Cumnock, where he was executed on 5 April 1685. His grave can be seen in the old cemetery there, adjacent to that of the famous Covenanter, Rev Alexander Peden.

The Greenockmains Bridge is crossed by the road, the Greenock Water flowing beneath it. The path, however, crosses the old Greenock Bridge, a sandstone structure that was erected in 1794, though plans for its erection had been passed in 1788. On the opposite side rises the wooded Castle Hill, perhaps indicating that an ancient fortress or hillfort once occupied its slopes.

Below the Castle Hill the Way leaves the B743 once more and makes its way across the field to join the north bank of the River Ayr. The river is then followed downstream to the mouth of the Whitehaugh Water. Beyond the confluence the Way comes back to the B743 near to North Limmerhaugh farm. A swing bridge can be used to cross the river here, to the site of South Limmerhaugh farm, but the Way keeps to the northern or right bank of the river. The bridge is rather precarious and care is needed if it is to be crossed.

The Way follows the River Ayr around the North Limmerhaugh Holm, leaving the proximity of the B743 behind. Just beyond the point of the holm is a tractor ford across to Tulloch Holm on the south side of the river. The ruins of the original North Limmerhaugh farm are found on the hillside above the west end of the holm. This was probably abandoned when the present farmhouse was erected further east. Below North Limmerhaugh ruins is a man-made pond with island. The pond has many bulrushes around it.

The route passes through some scrubby woodland, with numerous old but straggly trees on the slopes. The route keeps to the north side of the river, here and there leaving the waterside to keep to higher ground, for example along the West Braes. The riverside is followed down to the point of the holm near to the foot of the Tulloch Burn. This joins the Ayr just below a prominent tall cliff of clay. At this headland old fords existed, giving access to Tulloch Holm to the east and the old track to Crossbog farm on the south. West of the Tulloch Burn, on the southern side of the river, on the lands of Crossbog and Upper Heilar, is a regimented forestry plantation, occupying part of Airds Moss.

The River Ayr meanders through the glen here, generally heading south westerly. Walkers next reach the ruins of High Crook farm, now only shown on detailed maps as a sheepfold. This was in fact a house at one time, but its age is quite apparent as there is no sign of a chimney or fireplace. This would imply a very old stone and thatched black-house type of steading. The farm formerly had a well on the hillside immediately to its north. Today the ruins are surrounded by ferns.

On the south side of the river stood Crossbog farm. The remains of this and various stone dikes can be seen within the plantation. Below the farm, by the side of the river, is a stone cliff comprising beds of stratified rock, a hint of things to come. At Crossbog is the terminus of a forestry road that links westwards to a public road on the south side of the River Ayr, though it keeps quite distant from the river.

From High Crook the path makes its way up the slopes of the banking to by-pass the stratified rock cliff at the bend in the river. There is no way past the foot of the cliff and the high ground requires to be followed. The head of the banking is followed around to another meander, much of the upper ground of which was planted in trees in 2006. This meander could be known as the Middle Crook, and it has an interesting headland on it. If this is not the remains of some form of prehistoric fort, then early man missed the chance to utilise a naturally defensive flat headland. On the south side of the river a small burn that drains the forestry plantation tumbles into the Ayr by a waterfall dropping over stratified rocks. The Way bypasses part of the meander, keeping to higher ground, with views across the river to the ruins of Upper Heilar farm. This appears as quite a large dwelling with an array of doors and windows facing north-eastwards. There was at one time a very small whinstone quarry there.

The path is followed through some old straggly woods and some young plantations of 2006 towards Laigh Crook. These slopes are known as the Crook Brae. By the side of the river on the Upper Heilar side is a rock outcrop whose surface has been worn by the water, creating round holes, known in Scots lore as 'De'il's pots and pans'. At one time the river was crossed by a footbridge here, but this has long-since been washed away. Also across the river are some natural stone dikes, creating low weirs across the water. The path continues along the top of the banking to the ruins of Laigh Crook, another long-abandoned farmstead.

Laigh Crook is located at the head of another large meander in the river. The ruins indicate a traditional Scottish long-house, measuring approximately 90 feet by 18 feet. Unlike High Crook, this ruin had a hearth in the centre of the building, the two side stones of which still rise out of the ground. At the west end of the ruin the former byre is the most complete, no doubt as it was used by the farmer longer than the house. From Laigh Crook an old track leads north to Merkland farm and to the B743, the Way following this as far as the Merkland Burn.

Just beyond Laigh Crook the river tumbles over two waterfalls, the first one just downstream from the ruins. This is little more than a sill across the water, but the tumbling river makes a constant noise. The headland at the end of the haugh has views of the wooded Peel Craigs on the southern side of the river. The River Ayr takes a sharp turn here, the deep pool being a noted salmon fishing spot. After turning the corner the river splits around a fair-sized island, on which grow a number of trees, free from grazing sheep.

On the north side of the river, next to the island, is a rocky outcrop that is covered with trees, brambles, ivy and hazel. Although a natural feature, it is out of place where it exists, and on the southern side are a number of massive blocks of rock that have fallen from it. On detailed maps this is shown as the Peel, a name that may have indicated that it was a place of defence at one time. The summit of the Peel is small, however, and it is unlikely to have been a castle site.

The lower of the Laigh Crook falls is located where the farther branch of the river, which has passed down the other side of the Peel Island, returns to join the right branch. Again this fall is little more than a sill crossing the river, but this one is larger and rougher than the upper falls.

The path follows the track north towards the Merkland Burn, crossed by a footbridge. The slopes on the north side of the river, below Merkland farm which can be seen, were planted with a variety of trees in 2006. On the south side of the river is Mid Heilar farm, still occupied, and known also as Glendale.

The path climbs up to the Castle Hill, which comprises a Norman motte hill and bailey. This is located on the neck of land between the River Ayr and the mouth of the Wyndy Burn, seventy feet above the river bed. Although thought to have been fortified as a place of defence, much of the landscape that formed the hill is totally natural, with steep slopes plummeting from the summit down to the river or tributaries. There are actually two rounded hilltops, separated by a wide open ditch. Most of the slopes are wooded, making it difficult to appreciate the full layout.

The Way crosses the Wyndy Burn near where it joins the River Ayr, and the path continues along the riverside, at the edge of the Hole Holm, to the foot of the Benthead Burn. On the right, shortly after crossing the Wyndy Burn, can be seen the remains of Hole farm, partially hidden amongst trees. Much of the lower stretches of the Wyndy Burn are today thickly wooded and natural in appearance, but in the early nineteenth century a limestone quarry and limestone mine existed.

Hole Holm is a wide and rich stretch of farmland. Walkers keep to the edge of the field. On the south side of the river is a wooded banking below Nether Heilar farm, as well as Cubs Holm, a small stretch of level ground by the riverside.

At the west end of Hole Holm walkers require to leave the riverside and climb through trees to circumnavigate a high cliff just beyond the mouth of the Benthead Burn. At one point a sheer vertical drop plummets from the pathside down to the river, which has to make a sharp left turn on striking the foot of the cliff. Beyond this the cliff drops slowly down to the Daldilling Holm. At one time there was a well partially down this slope.

At the southernmost point of Daldilling Holm is a deep pool, part of Sorn estate fishing policies, and noted for salmon. A steep cliff on the south side is covered with part of the Roughhaugh Wood. The Roughhaugh Holm – a nonsensical hybrid, for holm and haugh are two Scots words meaning much the same – lies on the south side of the river. On the slopes above the Daldilling Holm is Daldilling farm. At one time there was a small lairdship of Daldilling, and the Reid family owned it for many years. George Reid of Daldilling was one of the co-accused of the murder of the Earl of Cassillis in 1527. John Reid was noted in the seventeenth century for hunting down Covenanters. Based at Sorn Castle, he was responsible for killing George Wood, who lived at Tincornhill, a few hundred yards north of Daldilling.

At the west end of the holm the path passes a fairly large pool of water to the right, surrounded by trees. This was formed when an old limestone quarry was flooded, sometime prior to 1860. Immediately south of the pool was also an old coal pit, a few fragments of masonry indicating its whereabouts. A long pool of water lies in front of two old limekilns, the masonry walls of which survive. The right-hand kiln has partially collapsed, but the kilns were of a fair size.

The Way is followed alongside the river westwards, towards Waterside farm, which is actually located on the southern side of the river. The path circles the remains of Holhouse Mill. Reference to the mill is made in 1646, when John Campbell inherited it. The mill may have been an oatmeal mill at that time.

On the south side of the river, beyond Waterside farm, is Glenlogan House, its white walls visible from the riverside. Glenlogan stands on the site of Dalgain Castle, a small tower-house owned by the Mitchells. It was later known at Burnhead. By the middle of the seventeenth century this had been replaced by the centre block of the present house, to which wings and additions were made in the eighteenth and nineteenth centuries. It was at one time owned by Hugh Logan of that Ilk (1739-1802), the celebrated wit who was a contemporary of Robert Burns, and who had his main seat at Logan House, near Cumnock. When he died in 1802 the house was inherited by George Ranken of Whitehill who renamed it Glenlogan in Hugh's honour. It has passed through many hands over the centuries. At one time the house was owned by J. G. Stephen of Linthouse, who owned a shipyard in Govan. To assist in designing ship hulls he had a large marine testing tank built at Waterside farm, latterly converted into an agricultural slurry tank.

On the south side of the river is the Roughhaugh Wood. Here at one time was a tree associated with Rev Alexander Peden, the noted Covenanter, who hid there during the years of persecution. Different maps indicate its location at different places, but the chances of a tree from the seventeenth century still growing here are slim, and the author could find no sign of one, despite it still being marked on the present Ordnance Survey Pathfinder map. Older Two and a Half inch maps position the tree in The Glen, nearer to the Shiel Burn, but indicate that this was the site of the tree.

The Way follows the right bank of the Ayr to the Haggis Bank, the name of the wooded slope along the riverside. Another old limekiln can be seen here, its archway facing south. The high masonry wall above it has a couple of aged trees growing from gaps between the stones. Westwards from here the pathway follows the old trackway through the Dalgainbank Plantation towards Glenlogan Bridge. This was at one time the main access route to the mines and limeworks that existed on Holhouse Holm but today is little more than a narrow path through the trees. At the side of the river, alongside Dalgain Holm, are some massive old beech trees.

The Way leaves the old trackway before it reaches Glenlogan Bridge and strikes westwards, through a wood to join the B743 on Dalgain Brae, just above Dalgain Cottage.

Glenlogan Bridge is a steel slab and girder bridge, perched on stone abutments at either side of the river and a stone-built central pier. Locally it is known as Timmers Brig. The old bridge was erected in 1778, but only parts of the stone walls on the approaches are as old. A roadway alongside the river could be used to take one to the B743, at the foot of the steep slope known as Dalgain Brae, at the eastern end of the village of Sorn. Dalgain farm is located here, an L-shaped steading of single-storey stone buildings. If desired, pathways can be followed from

Sorn Inn

Glenlogan Bridge back down the south side of the river, into the southern part of Sorn at Holmhead and Stepends.

Sorn is an attractive village, though many of its older houses and buildings have been removed and modern houses built in their place, making the main street wider and more open than it once was. The New Bridge dates from 1871, built by George Reid of Catrine, and carries the B713 across the River Ayr and southwards to Catrine and Auchinleck. It replaced the old Coal Ford, which was located a few hundred yards upstream.

The Sorn Inn has long had a reputation for fine food and is a fine eighteenth century building. The village hall opposite was erected in 1954 and next to it is Sorn Primary School, erected in 1850 and topped by a wooden clock tower.

Of some antiquity is Sorn Parish Church, located at the west end of the village. This church was erected in 1656 and is therefore one of only two Parliamentarian churches in the county. A simple sandstone structure, it is distinguished by its lancet windows and three sets of exterior steps leading to different galleries. The church was rebuilt in 1826. During the summer months it is open to the public by arrangement as part of Scotland's Churches Scheme. On the gable wall facing the entrance to the kirkyard hangs a set of jougs, used at one time to lock malefactors around the neck. The Kirk Session minutes of 23 November 1698 note:

> Whilk day Jean MacLatchie was dilated by authority of two
> magistrates, James Farquhar of Gilmillscroft, and Adam
> Aird of Katarin, and was by them put in the jougges, from

the ringing of the first to the ringing of the third bell, and then appeared to be rebuked before the congregation, for profanation of the Sabbath.

Around the church is an old kirkyard, with a number of interesting old tombstones. A mural memorial on the church wall commemorates some children of Rev Lewis Balfour, minister of Sorn from 1806-29. He was the grandfather of Robert Louis Stevenson, the celebrated author, and it is reckoned that RLS got his middle name from this man.

Also on the wall of the kirk the memorial to George Wood can be found. He is celebrated as the last and youngest martyr for the Covenant. He was in the fields at Tincorn Hill when soldiers came upon him. He was asked a number of questions, and his answers were such that they decided to shoot him on the spot. The date of his execution was sometime in June 1688, a few months after Rev James Renwick, who was the last martyr to hang in Edinburgh. The old stone to Wood is located above the later memorial, itself now of some antiquity.

Within Sorn kirkyard the graves of local landowners can be found, such as the MacIntyres of Sorn Castle, one of who became

Sorn Parish Church

Lord Sorn at the Court of Session. Also interred within a fine gothic burial enclosure are the Buchanans of Catrinebank, managers at Catrine mill.

The former manse is located behind the old kirkyard, a fine building of the eighteenth century. It has two main floors, and a rather heavy moulded doorway.

Across the road from the Parish Church is the church hall, converted from a mill building. The mill was of some antiquity, being the mill of the barony, and was probably the original Dalgain Mill. Power was supplied by a breast paddle, and three pairs of stones were operated by it. Adjacent to the mill building is the Old Mill Garden, a small open area in which can be seen two millstones. The garden, which gives access to the River Ayr waterside adjacent to the bridge, was the object of BBC Scotland's 'Beechgrove Garden' hit squad in 1997.

The River Ayr Way makes its way along the Main Street of the village of Sorn. An alternative route, if you wish to avoid the village, is to follow the pathway along Sornbank Plantation. From Dalgain this path makes its way along the bank above the village for three quarters of a mile before dropping to the B743 at the side of Sorn Cemetery. Sornbank Plantation was cut down and replanted around 2000, since when the local community has been active in creating the path. The wood is reached through an oak kissing gate, on the right hand side of the B743, just after the road heading north to Blindburn farm. Carved wooden lips adorn the top of the gate and posts. The way is made underfoot, and along the path side have been planted a number of specimen trees, such as silver birch, gean, Japanese cherry, purple leaved birch, hornbeam, red oak, silver maple, Norway maple, Chinese rowan, whitebeam and other varieties. At present, whilst the trees are young, there are extensive views of the village below. Short paths drop from the main path down to the village. At the west end of the Sornbank Plantation the path drops down a narrow spur of land with a gully to the right, dropping to a minor burn. At the bottom is a short route linking the path with the main road by the side of the Old Manse stables. A footbridge is crossed and the path continues further through the wood to the west end of the village, at the New Cemetery. Information boards are located at the west end of the pathway, next to the cemetery car park.

From the church in Sorn, the River Ayr Way heads across Sorn Old Bridge. At the end of the Bridge is a painted guide-stone indicating Catrine, Auchinleck and Cumnock.

The Old Bridge is a fine twin arched structure, built of sandstone. Hump-backed, the narrow carriageway is still used by vehicles. The bridge dates from between 1736-51, during the time of Rev William Steel's ministry. Some of his congregation were drowned at one time and he organised a collection in order to fund the bridge.

The Way follows the minor road along the riverside before climbing up the brae towards an attractive sandstone cottage, distinguished by its three arched Georgian windows. Known as Kilnknow Cottage, it is part of the Sorn Castle estate policies, and probably dates from around 1850. From the gate next to the cottage one can look across the field and the hidden river towards the impressive pile of Sorn Castle, standing high on a cliff above the river. The castle is open to the public during the summer months.

The oldest part of Sorn Castle that survives today dates from the fifteenth century, a fact recorded on a later date stone that claims the original tower was erected in 1409. This square tower house is located at the southern corner of the building. An extension along the cliffside was added in the sixteenth century, distinguished by its corbelled parapet. Later extensions were added in 1793 (designed by William Railton), 1865 (designed by David Bryce) and 1907 (designed by Henry Clifford). At one time Sorn estate was owned by the Keith family, but in 1406 the heiress married a Hamilton of Cadzow. A later heiress took the castle to the Setons of Winton. It later became part of the larger Campbell of Loudoun Castle properties, Sorn being the dower house for a time, but it changed hands on a number of occasions and has since 1908 been the property of the MacIntyre family.

Overlooking the river is a castellated porch attached to the castle. Legend claims that at some point Sorn Castle could crumble and fall into the river, so when this addition was made it

Sorn Castle

was built freestanding, with no link onto the rest of the castle.

In the river below the castle is a curved weir, guiding water into a turbine house that supplied the castle with electricity. This is located next to a private suspension footbridge.

Next to the castle, at the foot of the Cleuch Burn, are the Curate's Steps, associated with the Curate, or Episcopal minister, of Sorn, who served in the church during the time of the Covenanters. When the years of persecution came to an end, the Curate was 'rabbled' and fled across the burn for his own safety. The bridge over the burn has a strange cottage at its western side. This is tall with a circular tower, the masonry rusticated. Sorn Castle was used as a garrison for government dragoons during the Covenanting period, and still to be seen in the castle are a drum and halbert from this period, as well as Sorn parish Covenanting banner.

The Way leaves the minor road through a kissing gate and enters the wood by the side of the road, to the south of Kilnknow cottage. It makes its way around the edge of the field overlooking the castle, known as Kilnknow Park, and reaches the highest point at the yard of Smiddyshaw farm. It then gradually drops down towards the side of the river once more, to the Foulsyke Wood. On the north side of the river, among the woods, is the Sorn Castle private burial ground.

Smiddyshaw has a strange sandstone-built tower, the purpose of which is not fully known. It may have been a windmill, but the workings have gone. By the riverside below Smiddyshaw are the remains of an old sandstone quarry, the sheer face of the quarry still visible at the waterside. From the top of the quarry a trackway up the hillside towards Smiddyshaw can still be made out on the ground.

The path follows the southern bank of the river westwards, through wooded slopes towards Daldorch House. The woods, Foulsyke Wood and Northbank Wood, are mature, and are full of Scots Pine, Beech and other trees. The undergrowth comprises of rhododendron, which grows wildly, having spread from Sorn Castle policies. A small stream is crossed by a bridge near the riverside, after which the path keeps to the edge of the River Ayr. Near Daldorch House the Way passes an old stone-built shelter that formed part of the policies of Daldorch. This was probably used by residents of the house to have picnics, or else to shelter whilst fishing in the large pool of the river that exists here. Old maps indicate it was a Summer House.

On the northern side of the river is a level flood plain, or holm as they are known in Ayrshire, with the ruins of Waulkmill.

Also rising above and steeply wooded is Sorn Hill.

Daldorch House was at one time the home of the managers of Catrine mill, Archibald Buchanan, *piere et fils*. Archibald Senior had been an apprentice of Sir Richard Arkwright, the famous Derbyshire mill-owner. Another owner was Charles Howatson of Dornal (1833-1918), who later built Glenbuck House. Daldorch was also known as Catrinebank for a time, but it has for some time taken the older name of Daldorch. The original block of the house dates from around 1812, but in the early Victorian period a sizeable extension was added to the east, two and a half storeys plus basement in height (designed by Edinburgh architect, Thomas Hamilton). Since 1998 the house has formed part of Daldorch House School, operated by the National Autistic Society. The main block of the house was extended considerably with modern residential wings and separate houses in 1997-8 (designed by MEB Partnership), all surrounded by a secure fence. Here, within eleven acres of property, the society provides residential care for 40 children aged from five to nineteen years.

The footpath follows the large meander of the River Ayr to the north of Daldorch. The opposite bank of the river rises steeply for one hundred feet to a minor road above. As this holm formed part of Daldorch's policies a few specimen trees can be seen, including old beech, oak and a yew tree.

At the west end of Daldorch holm the path reaches a large concrete weir across the river. This was the main dam that directed water down through Catrine Voes towards the large mill complex that once existed in the centre of the village. Today the weir is partially used, for water is still redirected from the river, but it does not drive anything any more. In the late spring floods salmon can be spotted leaping up the ladder at the dam.

Just beyond the footbridge is the former stable block of Daldorch, extended in 2005-6 to form part of Daldorch House School.

Below the weir the Way crosses a footbridge, bringing one into the village of Catrine. The footbridge was at one time fiercely guarded as a private access route to Daldorch House, as can be seen by the gate and spikes, but today is open as part of the Way. The bridge, which has a wooden deck, is made from steel lattice work, and was constructed by P. & R. Fleming & Company of Glasgow.

On crossing the footbridge one walks past the bowling green and through a wrought iron gate into the Catrine Voes local nature reserve. The Voes (or reservoirs) were created as part of Catrine mill complex, and was where the waters were stored from the

River Ayr prior to passing through underground lades to the big wheel. Today they are havens of peace, spots where wildlife such as swans, kingfishers, otters, water voles and dippers thrive.

Catrine Bowling Club's green is located on the site of St Cuthbert's Chapel. Little is known about this place of worship, but the name survives in the adjacent street name and in St Cuthbert's Holm, or Culbert Holm as it is better known to the locals. The bowling club was founded in 1872.

South of the voes, on a large meander of the river, is the Glen Catrine bonded warehouse complex, the largest independent bottling plant in Scotland. This was the site of the bleachworks, established in 1820, but since 1974 the large sheds and buildings have been used for the blending and bottling of whisky and other spirits. Glen Catrine is part of the Loch Lomond Distillery Company, and brands such as Glen Catrine and High Commissioner whisky (Britain's fifth most popular whisky at the time of writing) are produced here, as well as Glen's vodka (Britain's second highest selling vodka). The firm produces in excess of 36½ million bottles of whisky, vodka, gin, rum and brandy per annum. A small waterfall is located at the corner of the river, below Lindsay Bank.

On the north side of the voes is St Cuthbert's Street, an attractive line of houses built at the foot of a steep bank. A public pathway up through the back of the houses leads to the minor roadway linking Catrine with Sorn Castle. At one point on the road, perched on the edge of the embankment, is the tall obelisk that forms Catrine War Memorial.

At the west end of the main reservoir the Way follows a pathway down to the Laigh Road, back at the side of the River Ayr. Over the wall to the left of this pathway can be seen an open section of the former lade where the overflow from the mill race returned to the river. The path then heads west along Laigh Road, by the side of the river, to Ayr Street. On the opposite bank of the river is the playing fields.

At the gusset of roads, the Way keeps to the right, following Wood Street to Mill Square. Ayr Street could quite as easily have been followed by the riverside to the Ayr Bridge and St Germain Street. This rather foreign-sounding street gets its name from the patron saint of weavers. The bridge crossing the River Ayr dates from 1906, replacing an older hump-backed bridge.

St Germain Street is the shopping centre of the village, the tall sandstone building being the former co-operative, erected in 1903 to plans by Gabriel Andrew. At the west end of the street is the Royal Bank of Scotland, erected in 1873 to plans by Peddie &

Kinnear. The other buildings are less distinguished, being much abused traditional Scots vernacular buildings, apart from the modern, but traditional in style, block of houses erected in 1994-5 by George Reid & Sons to plans by Meikle-Kleboe architects. A number of local shops, inns, post office and café can be found here.

Catrine dates from 1786, when the local landowner, Sir Claud Alexander of Ballochmyle decided to set up a weaving community on the lines of New Lanark. He obtained the services of David Dale to assist, and soon a large mill building was erected in the centre of what is now Mill Square. The power for the mill came from the river, and on 31 March 1828 this was increased when the famous Catrine Big Wheel started powering the complex. This was a pair of water-powered breast-bucket mill wheels that could produce 500 horsepower, probably the largest in the world at the time, and as a result it became something of a tourist attraction,

Catrine Parish Church

49

with tours coming to the village from all around. The wheels even inspired poetry from Robert Wright in 1836:

> *Two mighty wheels the work then undertook,*
> *Of iron formed – and of gigantic look:*
> *Huge Herculeans, of man's work the chief,*
> *Whose just description far exceeds belief;*
> *Majestic grandeur, strength and power combined,*
> *Declare them offspring of some mighty mind.*

The wheels were erected by Sir William Fairbairn of Manchester. Each wheel was 50 feet in diameter and twelve feet in width, and had 120 buckets to hold water. They turned at three revolutions per minute, powered by 240 tons of water per minute. The wheels became redundant when the new mill was erected in 1946, and electricity was introduced to the mill complex with the erection of a power station.

A few older buildings from the time of the first mill can still be found in Catrine, but much of it has been rebuilt over the years. Of interest is the parish church, perched high on the hillside. This is a most attractive building, dating from 1792, having been built by Sir Claud Alexander as a chapel of ease for his mill workers, preventing the need to walk to the parish church in Sorn. The architect of the building is not known. It has attractive lancet-arched windows, and a pediment over the main entrance, with carved swags and above it a cupola bell-tower. To the west of the church, on the steep hillside, is a churchyard. Catrine Parish Church was created a quoad sacra church in 1871. It underwent renovations in 1874, and again more recently. The church is open to the public on request as part of Scotland's Churches Scheme.

The former Free Church still survives, now converted into a large house. The church was erected in 1845 and latterly served as a Congregational Church from 1960 until 2002. Near to it, behind the presbytery, is the timber Roman Catholic Chapel of St Joseph, opened in May 1962. Further to the west, on the corner of Ballochmyle Street with Mauchline Road, is the former United Presbyterian Church, designed by James Ingram, and erected in 1836. This is now the parish church hall.

From the Ayr Bridge one can look eastward towards Nether Catrine House, now lost amongst a line of later houses known as Stewart Place. Nether Catrine was a fine old Scots laird's house of 1682, distinguished by its pedimented frontage which faces the opposite way from the street. The house predated the surrounding

A.M. Brown Institute

village, and at one time was owned by Professor Dugald Stewart (1753-1828). His father, Professor Matthew Stewart (1717-85) was the Chair of Mathematics at the University of Edinburgh and was succeeded by Dugald. However, he was later to become Professor of Moral Philosophy, and became a celebrated metaphysician. Professor Dugald Stewart was a friend of Robert Burns, and he invited the poet to a dinner here on 23 October 1786. Among the guests was Lord Daer, son of the Earl of Selkirk, resulting in Burns versifying on the first time he 'dinner'd wi' a lord':

> *This wot ye all whom it concerns:*
> *I, Rhymer Rab, alias Burns,*
> *October twenty-third,*
> *A ne'er to be forgotten day,*
> *Sae far I sprauchled up the brae,*
> *I dinner'd wi' a Lord.*

Burns was to spend many evenings with Professor Stewart in Edinburgh after this visit. There is a large monument to the Professor on Edinburgh's Calton Hill, designed by W. H. Playfair.

In Mill Square a stone sculpture representing Catrine's history can be seen, based on the big wheel. Walkers should follow Bridge Street south from the Square towards the river once more, passing on the left Bridge Lane Day Centre. The River Ayr is crossed by the pedestrian Timmer (from timber) Bridge. This name is somewhat dated, for the present bridge is made from steel and was opened on 3 May 1879, replacing what had been a wooden bridge. The steel bridge cost £139 9s 3d to build and was presented to the village by Archibald Buchanan of James Finlay & Co. After being washed away in a flood in 1966, it was rebuilt eighteen inches higher up. Looking back one can see Abernethy Cottage, which has an attractive frontage to the river, whereas the side facing Bridge Lane is rather plain. On the gable, which is an unusual mansard style with heavy mouldings at the foot of the chimneys, can be made out the lower, much simpler gable, of the original cottage. The cottage was rebuilt in its present style in 1886.

On the southern side of the bridge is the Ballochmyle sandstone A. M. Brown Institute, now used as Catrine community centre. The institute was erected in 1898 to plans by Robert Ingram, the funds of £2000 being supplied by A. M. Brown (d. 1906), director of James Finlay & Co., which ran the cotton works. The institute has a squat octagonal clock tower, though its location in this quiet corner of the village prevents it from being seen as often as it might. Within the institute are a few old relics of Catrine's historical past, including the bell from the old mill, another from the Institute (cast in Glasgow by John C. Wilson, 1899), a bust of A. M. Brown, and the war memorial plaque from the former Catrine Junior Secondary School.

An alternative route from the Ayr Bridge at the east end of St Germain Street can be followed to here. On crossing the bridge one should turn right into Newton Street, following it in a south-westerly direction. A few hundred yards along the street a path strikes to the right, joining the south side of the River Ayr, which it follows along to Institute Avenue.

3. CATRINE to STAIR

A footbridge crosses the Bogend Burn, to the west of the A. M. Brown Institute in Catrine, leading onto Catrine Holm, the name of the large extent of flat ground on the south side of the river. A roadway makes its way alongside the river, with some modern bungalows to the left (including Cygnet House, erected in 1995), heading for Catrine Sewage Works. The path keeps to the river bank, following the side of the river in a wide sweep around Catrine Holm, before turning at the foot of the wooded Brae of Ballochmyle. Views can be made from Catrine Holm north over the river to the parish church, perched on the side of the hill overlooking the village.

The large sandstone house on the north side of the river is Ayrbank House, at one time the home of the manager in the cotton mill. The original part of the house is constructed of the local pink sandstone and is located to the north of the large Victorian red sandstone additions. It is a Grade B listed building and has a Victorian summerhouse overlooking the river. On the opposite side of the road from Ayrbank, and visible from the Way, are the former Free Church (now a private house), and the former United Presbyterian Church.

A pipe crosses the River Ayr part of the way along Catrine Holm, carrying sewage from the north side of the river. The pipe forms a small weir, over which the river tumbles. On the north side of the river can be seen an old masonry wall, supporting the river bank. Behind this was the exit tunnel of the mill race for Catrine Mill, the water running westwards before returning to the river. The exit can be seen near to the ruins of Burnfoot Bridge, itself, at one time, an ornamental bridge on an approach to

Ballochmyle House, which stands on the wooded hill above.

The Braes of Ballochmyle is a name known to Burnsians, for the bard composed a poem in honour of Miss Wilhelmina Alexander of Ballochmyle (1756-1843), in which he praised the beauties of the Braes of Ballochmyle, as the wooded slopes on the west side of the river are known. These are steep and have outcrops of soft sandstone among the trees and rhododendron bushes.

Miss Alexander was the daughter of Claud Alexander of Newtoun and sister of Claud Alexander of Ballochmyle. She was spotted by Burns whilst he was out walking, and he composed a song in her honour, entitled 'The Lass of Ballochmyle'. He sent this to her in November 1786 but she ignored the letter. Burns was later to write that she was 'too fine a lady to notice so plain a compliment.' However, Miss Alexander never married, and it is said that she long cherished the letter and poem until her death. She is buried somewhere below Glasgow Airport!

> *With careless step I onward stray'd,*
> *My heart rejoic'd in Nature's joy,*
> *When, musing in a lonely glade,*
> *A maiden fair I chanc'd to spy.*
> *Her look was like the morning's eye,*
> *Her air like Nature's vernal smile.*
> *Perfection whisper'd, passing by:—*
> *'Behold the lass o' Ballochmyle!'*

Ballochmyle House still stands on the top of the hill on the opposite side of the river. Ballochmyle was long owned by the Alexander family, having acquired the estate in 1785 from the Whitefoords, who had lost financially with the crash of the Ayr Bank in 1772. Claud Alexander (1753-1809) was paymaster-general in the East India Company and it was he who acquired the estate. The house had actually been erected in 1760 by Allan Whitefoord, on the site of an old tower house, to plans by John Adam, elder brother of the more famous Robert. In 1886-90 massive additions to the front were added in sandstone to Jacobean plans by Hew Montgomerie Wardrop, with an impressive armorial doorway, celebrating the raising of the Alexander family to a baronetcy in 1886.

During the Second World War Ballochmyle was requisitioned and converted into an emergency hospital. The house acted as nurses' quarters for a time, until the dry rot became so bad that they had to move out. In the grounds west of the mansion extensive blocks of wards were laid out. It was at Ballochmyle Hospital that the first ever plastic surgery took place, developed to treat victims of bombings. The hospital was finally closed in August 2000. The roof of the house was removed in 2005 as part of a scheme to restore the house as flats.

The path follows the River Ayr in a southerly direction, passing the sewage works on the left. At times there is a smell from the evaporating water. At the southern extremity of Catrine Holm the river takes a sharp right, having hit a high headland. The path climbs up the steep slopes to the top of the cliff, before heading west along the cliff-top. There are a number of fine old beeches and other trees here. The path then descends gently down the other side of the point, into a wooded valley, with the river far down to the west. The path continues through woodland before passing under the large Howford Bridge, which carries the A76 high above.

The Howford Bridge was erected 1961-2 to plans by F. A. MacDonald and Partners. The old road was too twisty and difficult for modern traffic, so it was decided to build a new road and bridge, crossing the gorge at the level of the surrounding countryside. Two massive concrete arches carry supporting pillars on which the concrete road deck is held high above the glen. On the arch is some graffiti painted by rather daring vandals!

Shortly after passing under the Howford Bridge one arrives at the original Howford Bridge. This probably dates from 1750, and it has been speculated that the date 1751 at the cup and ring markings was carved there by one of the masons involved in building the bridge. The bridge has two arches and triangular cutwaters. The arch rings comprise dressed stone; the spandrels are of rubble. At one time Howford Toll Cottage sat on the eastern side of the bridge, but was removed to improve the road lines.

Tradition claims that James Armour (d. 1798), father-in-law of Robert Burns, was involved in the construction of this bridge. He is known to have been a master mason and a number of bridges and buildings from this period are ascribed to him. At times otters can be seen in the river.

When the old Howford Bridge is crossed one leaves Sorn parish and enters Mauchline. The original line of the A76 is followed for 1100 yards before heading due west, crossing a stile and following a path down through the Kingencleugh gorge. The stretch of old road is still accessible to vehicles from the present A76, just over one mile from Mauchline Cross. Cars can be parked by the roadside and walks made from here.

Howford Bridge

From the Old Howford Bridge one walks along the former road. On the right is a belt of woodland, whereas to the left the land drops down to the Holm Field, with the River Ayr sweeping around the holm, or floodplain. Every May, this field is used by Sorn Parish Agricultural Society to house Catrine Show, a popular event with local farmers. The Society was founded in 1872.

Just as the road and the river appear to part company, two tall sandstone abutments can be seen to either side of the road. These are the remains of a narrow footbridge that at one time crossed the road, part of an extensive network of private paths in what were the policies of Ballochmyle estate. Around 150 yards beyond the former bridge is the stile across the fence to the left. In the wood to the right is South Lodge cottage, formerly one of Ballochmyle House's gate lodges.

A footpath angles down the edge of the field towards a footbridge across a little stream. On the slopes to the left are other paths snaking through the woods, climbing to a high sandstone promontory between the little burn and the River Ayr. Some of the paths are extremely exposed, and great care is needed, especially with children and dogs, as there are vertical cliffs of great height here.

In the trees to the right, just over the bridge, can be found a magnificent example of prehistoric rock art. A vertical sandstone cliff is covered with numerous cup and ring markings, as well as other strange carvings, which are thought to date from the Bronze Age. These carvings were only rediscovered in 1986 when the trees here were cut down, and some locals recognised them as being of national importance. Most cup and ring markings elsewhere are to be found on horizontal rocks, leading to some speculations as to what they may have been used for, such as moulds for jewellery, but as these markings are on a natural cliff, these theories can now be discredited. These cup and ring markings are reckoned to be one of Britain's ten best examples. Sadly, there are a few examples of later rock-art on the cliffs, though one of the early examples of graffito dates from 1751!

A number of other sandstone cliffs in the area are covered with carvings of a later period – names and initials carved into the rocks by passing youths or walkers. Thousands of these exist, the soft sandstone being a suitable rock for the carvers to leave their mark. Some of the names include dates, in some cases themselves being of some antiquity.

Of more interest, however, is the spot known as the Fisher's Tryst. A group of regular fishermen in the glen were called up to fight in the war. They met at the Tryst prior to leaving, and vowed to meet once more on their return. However, a number of the men were killed, and those who made it back to Howford had the names of those lost in action carved into the rock.

Obvious to the walker in front is the massive sandstone structure of the Ballochmyle Viaduct, over which the Glasgow to Dumfries railway line passes. The viaduct is a major feat of engineering, erected between 1846-8 for the Glasgow, Paisley, Kilmarnock & Ayr Railway, later to become the Glasgow and South Western Railway. The viaduct has seven arches across the gorge, but the large central arch is obviously the most spectacular. This has a span of 181 feet and is reckoned to be the longest masonry railway arch ever built. The viaduct still earns a place as a Guinness World Record. From the River Ayr to the height of the rails is 167 feet. The lesser arches are 50 feet wide, and the piers are 38 feet wide.

The engineers Grainger and Miller of Edinburgh were responsible for the design, which was unlike any other viaduct built at that time. The foundation stone was laid on 5 September 1846 and a massive scaffold of Baltic pine logs was used to support the masonry as it was constructed. Each of the 1200 logs was fourteen inches in diameter. Four hundred men were involved in the construction and, unusually for the time, there were no fatalities. The keystone was laid on 8 April 1847 and the final stone on 12 March 1848. The bridge has an inscription on it that was never completed, so today it still reads 'The last stone of this structure was laid on the .... day of ....'

From the viaduct the path descends down to the riverside and makes its way through attractive woods to the west. Nine hundred yards downstream from the viaduct are the remains of an old dam, two blocks of masonry still visible in the middle of the river and parts of the cliff on the opposite side showing mortises cut out for the dam to tie into. At the corner of the path can be seen a tunnel from where the lade commenced, one of the finest engineering structures on the river. Remains of the lade survive, at various parts passing through tunnels cut through the natural rock. Much of this is open and care should be taken if one wishes to look into them.

The path is gradually squeezed between sandstone cliffs and the river, at one point near to the foot of the Kingencleugh Burn the walker needs to scramble precariously at the riverside. If the river is in spate there is little alternative but to retrace one's steps and make a different route above the cliffs.

If the steep embankment is climbed one can see the ruins of Kingencleugh Castle, an old ruin by the side of the wood to the south-west of the present Kingencleugh House. The castle probably dates from 1600, and was erected by the Campbell family. The building was originally L-plan, but today only one wing survives, rising to a complete gable. The celebrated Reformer, Rev John Knox, is thought to have visited the castle's predecessor and preached here in the middle of the sixteenth century.

Kingencleugh House is the seat of the Hagart-Alexander family, Baronets of Ballochmyle. The house is an attractive Georgian building, possibly erected in 1765 by Robert Campbell and added to in 1777. In 1957 the house was restored by Sir Claud Hagart-Alexander to plans by Mervyn Noad of Glasgow. It was at this time the porch with an armorial panel and elephant finial on the gable were added.

Just beyond the foot of the Kingencleugh Burn the river gorge ends, and the countryside opens up for a bit. A track can be followed along the side of the mill lade towards Haugh Farm. To the left the track ends where it drops into the River Ayr, there being an old ford here which gave access to Damhead and Barwhillan cottages on the south side of the river, both now ruins. An alternative to following the track, a path by the riverside can be taken towards the remains of Haugholm, next to the bridge. Originally the river was crossed here by a ford, with a suspension footbridge alongside. A road bridge was erected in its place but was swept away in the floods of August 1966. The present bridge was erected in 1967.

There has been a mill of sorts at the Haugh for many centuries, the earliest reference to one being in 1527 when the Ayr was harnessed to drive a corn mill. The present lades and works were used to drive a former woollen mill that stood where the cottages are. The mill was three storeys in height and had workers' cottages alongside.

By the side of the road at Haugh Farm is an old corn mill, built of sandstone rubble, but totally stripped out inside and reused as a garage and store. At the southern end can still be seen the gable where the millwheel was powered by the surviving lade. The building is thought to have been erected in the early nineteenth century and was where the original Mauchline curling stones were made. Old accounts make reference to this as the 'icestone mill'. It operated until around 1910 when Andrew Kay moved to larger premises in Mauchline, taking over a former snuff box factory. The manufacture of curling stones is something that still takes place in Mauchline, a unique industry whose product is exported all over the world.

The farmhouse at Haugh Farm has an inscribed lintel, though unfortunately the third initial is covered by a lamp. Still visible is 'WB[?] 1772'. The Way makes its route past the house, then onto the public road, heading towards Mauchline.

Opposite the Haugh farm, the Way follows a roadway that makes its way down to the former Ballochmyle Creamery building, located between a wooded embankment and the River Ayr. The creamery was established in the nineteenth century and the original building is quite distinctive, being designed in a Swiss cottage fashion, three storeys in height, with a tall central ventilating tower, originally sporting a flagpole. Around the creamery building were extensive gardens, adorned with busts on pedestals. Some of these commemorated members of the McCrone family, who owned the creamery for a time. The creamery was later taken over by the Jurgens margarine company, based in Germany, who produced 'Sea Foam' margarine here. The creamery was closed in 1946. The buildings were later converted into an optical works, where UKO Optical made glasses. At the time of writing the original creamery buildings and later corrugated iron and steel sheds are abandoned, awaiting a further use, perhaps as houses.

One of the most noted members of the McCrone family was Guy McCrone (1898-1977), who found some fame as an author. He was born at Birkenhead and spent some time at Mauchline, but was educated at Glasgow and Cambridge before studying

singing in Vienna. On his return to Scotland he was active in
theatres, and was jointly, with James Bridie, responsible for
founding the Citizen's Theatre in Glasgow. His trilogy of novels
on the lives of the Moorhouse family, known as the *Wax Fruit
Trilogy*, published in 1947, was his most successful, and remains in
print. Other works produced by him were less successful.

Near the gates of the creamery, adjacent to Haughbank
House, the Way makes its way through a steel kissing gate and
immediately up the past the side of the house to the field at the
top of the banking. From here it strikes west, entering the wood
where the path becomes more obvious again. It reaches the edge
of the field to the south of Mauchline Creamery, here seen as a
large corrugated iron shed. The path skirts the edge of the field,
between the fence and a beech hedge and reaches the public road
(Barskimming Road) next to two houses at the creamery entrance.

Mauchline Creamery was erected in 1936-8 in the Bent Field.
The buildings were designed by Alex Mair, and were originally
typical modern 1930s in style. However, most of the
ornamentation has been removed as the creamery has been rebuilt
and extended over the years. Today the creamery is used as a
packaging depot for cheese.

The Way follows Barskimming Road northwards, past a
milestone indicating that Mauchline is one mile to the north,
whereas Schaw is 4¾ miles to the south west. To the left is a pine
wood behind a sandstone estate wall. The North East Lodge of
Barskimming estate is passed on the left, and soon one arrives at
Woodlands farm.

Although not part of the River Ayr Way, the interested walker
can make his way down the road towards what is known as
Barskimming Old Bridge, passing the waste water treatment works
on the left. On the right is a gateway leading to Barskimming
estate, marked as private. This gives access to the Sandwalk
Plantation, where an estate path makes its way along the top of
the wooded cliff towards Barskimming Kennels. On the right,
carved from the solid sandstone, is a small cave with an arched
doorway. This is just one of many strange caves and summer
houses that either exist or formerly existed on the Barskimming
estate. This was at one time used by a Thomas MacMinn as a
milking house.

Barskimming Old Bridge dates from the eighteenth century. It
is a single-arched structure, the arch being 100 feet across, the arch
ring and spandrels being of dressed stone. The parapets have been
repaired numerous times over the years, a result of vehicles hitting
the sides. On the southern side of the bridge can be seen the

heads of various steel tie-rods.

At one time there was a double-storey cottage on the north side of the bridge, almost built into the cliff-side. Known as Bridge House, it was demolished around 1945-50. At one time this was the home the Kemp family, of which the daughter Kate Kemp was known to Robert Burns. One day he is said to have come here to visit her, only to discover that she was out. Instead he crossed the bridge and walked along Bridge Holm. As he walked he is thought to have composed his poem, 'Man was made to mourn'.

Upstream from the southern side of Barskimming Old Bridge is Barskimming Mill, formerly powered by water from a dam 400 yards further up the river. The mill buildings, which at the time of writing are in a ruinous condition, comprise of a variety of 2- 3- and 4-storey brick buildings, some of which have sandstone quoins. The lade was widened and deepened in 1834. The mill was rebuilt by William Alexander of Ballochmyle around 1893 following a fire, and had two water wheels and six pairs of stones. Two of these were for shelling, one was for finishing oatmeal and the last pair was for milling flour and provender. In recent years the mill buildings were used as a small engineering works.

One of the last millers at Barskimming Mill was James Andrew, who introduced many innovations. He lit the premises with coal gas, and on the first night the building was thus illuminated, he held a ball for the locals. However, the lamps ran out of gas before the dance was over, and the guests had to leave in the dark! Within his house at the mill he installed a pipe organ, powering it from the mill. On his death the organ was sold to the parish church in Mauchline, where it remained in use until 1912. It was then transferred to Patna church. Andrew spent much of his time directing the erection of other corn mills. He invented a lever friction hoist, a self-feeding travelling saw bench and other devices used in mills. He was the first to adopt double-shelling oats, using two pairs of shelling stones.

Barskimming House stands on a high cliff directly above the River Ayr. The present mansion is a three storey classical building, erected in 1883. The house stands on an ancient site, for the lands of Barskimming were granted to William Reid by Robert II in 1377. The Reids remained in ownership for many centuries, but by 1691 the estate had been sold to the Millers. Sir Thomas Miller, 1st Baronet (1717-90), was Lord President of the Court of Session. He rebuilt Barskimming House in 1770, and greatly enhanced the estate by creating stable blocks, follies and grottoes. It is said that Barskimming House was one of the finest houses in

Scotland at that time, but it was destroyed in a fire in March 1882. Sir Thomas's son, Sir William, was a Lord of Session, taking his title Lord Glenlee (1755-1846).

On the north side of the River Ayr is Barskimming Stables, a white-painted courtyard building erected in 1774. A pend through a tower gives access to the courtyard, and the building is distinguished by its Georgian paned windows and Venetian windows. The block has been converted into dwellings.

Linking the two Barskimming buildings is Barskimming New Bridge, erected in 1763 by Sir Thomas Miller. This rises from the perpendicular cliff on either side of the river, spanned by a single arch about 60 feet above the level of the water. At either end are stone obelisks and the parapets comprise stone balusters.

After passing through a variety of owners, Barskimming was purchased by Robert Jack Dunlop (1857-1938). In 1946 the estate passed to Thomas Dunlop Galbraith (1891-1985), who was raised to the peerage as Lord Strathclyde in 1955. His son, Sir Thomas Galbraith (1917-82) was MP for Hillhead in Glasgow, but he died before his father. The title passed to the first Lord's grandson, Thomas Galbraith, 2nd Lord Strathclyde, who is the Conservative Leader of the House of Lords.

During the period 1939-1957 Barskimming House was requisitioned for the War Office, during which time it operated as a home for Catholic boys. An account of some of the brutality endured by the boys was written by William Dyer, entitled *My memoirs of a Mansion fit for a Lady but not for me.*

The Barskimming estate is private, and the River Ayr Way makes a detour to avoid the immediate policies around the house. At Woodside farm the Way strikes west into the fields, following a track westwards for 850 yards. The route then turns north, heading for the trees that grow around a deep pool of water. This was formed when a former sandstone quarry, for which Mauchline was famous, was flooded. Passing alongside the trees, the route then turns west, following a little burn towards the Kipplemoss Plantation.

The Kipplemoss Plantation is a large wood of mixed trees, though mainly pine and birch. The path makes its way through the middle of the wood, heading for the Muir farm, with its silos. At this point views can be made north-eastwards to Mauchline and the Burns Monument of 1896-8.

At the far end of the wood the Way follows the fence up to a track linking Muir and Highaird farms. This is actually known as Barskimming Old Avenue. An old wood is followed to the west, and then along the northern edge of Paulshill Plantation. En route the path crosses the Mauchline Burn, marking the parish boundary between Mauchline and Tarbolton. This stream is actually known locally by the rather grandiose name of 'River Chalk'. The path continues alongside Paulshill Plantation, from where views can be made northwards to Failford House and other buildings within what was Smithstone estate. Smithstone House is now known as Old Auchenfail Hall, but it is hidden within the trees.

The Way arrives at the northern driveway into Barskimming estate. To the south, a few hundred yards along the drive, is Burnfoot Cottage, a gatehouse to the estate. The cottage is an attractive old building, with a small pediment on top of pilasters, as well as ogival-headed windows. The cottage is perched on top of a sandstone rock, next to an old bridge crossing the last stretches of the Mauchline Burn. Carved from the rock on which the cottage stands are two rooms, formerly used as a byre and storehouse. Within one of these is a fireplace and chimney, most of it carved from the sandstone. Below the cottage a second stone bridge crosses the stream, before crossing the River Ayr by way of the steel plate and girder Burnfoot Bridge, from where access can be made to Stairaird House on the opposite side, above Stairaird Bank.

Stairaird House is a rather fine country house of manageable proportions. A mixture of Georgian and Gothic styles, the house was erected around 1770 and is now the home of Richard Vernon, Depute Lord Lieutenant of Ayrshire and Arran. His wife is the daughter of Lord Glenarthur, a previous owner of the house. Stairaird is distinguished by its ogival arched windows on the first floor, and fine dentil cornicing at the wallheads. The main entrance faces east, gazing from its elevated hilltop position over the wooded grounds of Barskimming estate (of which the house was once part) towards Barskimming itself. Burnfoot Bridge links Stairaird on the south side of the river with Paulshill on the north, although the river travels in all sorts of directions hereabouts. In fact it flows North, South, West and East all within one mile of each other.

From Barskimming the river has meandered through wooded gorges for about two and a half miles. West of Barskimming New Bridge the river circles Netheraird Holm on the north bank, followed by Thirdpart Holm, the latter of which is afforested and located on the southern side of the river. Another large meander sees the River making its way around Lockharts Hill, also wooded, and located on the northern side of the river.

The River Ayr Way follows the northern drive of Barskimming estate from Paulshill Plantation towards a cottage alongside the B743 (Ayr to Mauchline road), just to the east of Failford village. This cottage was a gatehouse, and though it would seem to be the northern one for Barskimming it was in fact the western gate for Smithston House, the main road being straightened around the house, leaving it stranded on the 'wrong' side of the road.

Just short of the main road the Way strikes south into the woods above Woodside Cottage. The path drops through the trees towards the rear of the cottage, from where it heads westwards by the side of the river once more. On the south side can be seen a high sandstone cliff, the lines in the bedrock being formed when desert sand dunes were compressed millions of years ago.

On the hillside above the river stands the cottage of Woodhead. It was here that the Covenanting martyr, William Shillilaw, was shot around July 1685 by Lieutenant Lewis Lauder, from the garrison at Sorn Castle. Shillilaw was only eighteen years of age and worked at Stairhead (perhaps Stairaird). Lauder went there after killing Shillilaw, and was planning killing the employer but his soldiers refused, and he was reprieved. Shillilaw's grave can be seen in Tarbolton kirkyard.

At the west end of Woodside Holm the Way returns to the woods. The path has to climb up to by-pass a large sandstone bluff that rises sheer out of a deep pool in the river. On the other side a descent is made to the riverside once more, picking up a fisherman's path. This is followed along the riverside towards Failford. Here and there can be seen steel ladders down from the path to the riverside. The path gradually rises towards the B743, which links Ayr and Mauchline. It makes its way along the top of a cliff, between the road and the river, before joining the road just east of the village of Failford.

Failford is a small community that is located at the mouth of the Water of Fail. The ford has long-since been replaced by a bridge. The village started around 1800 when Alexander Cooper of Smithston left money for the erection of almshouses for the poor of Mauchline and Tarbolton parishes. The oldest part of the community is a row of single-storey cottages on the south, or river, side of the main road. One of these cottages has been converted into the Failford Inn, an attractive village pub where meals and refreshments are available. The inn also has its own real ale brewery, producing Windiegoat ale amongst other products. There are no other facilities in the village other than a public telephone box.

It was near the mouth of the Water of Fail that Robert Burns and his sweetheart, 'Highland' Mary Campbell parted company on

Failford

14 May 1786. Burns and Jean Armour had separated for a time, and he had fallen in love with Mary Campbell, who worked as a dairy maid at Coilsfield House. Burns was planning on emigrating to Jamaica, and had asked Mary to go with him and be his wife. Mary and he swapped Bibles by the mouth of the Fail, which is seen by some as indicating a form of marriage. Mary went to Greenock to prepare for the move, but she died there in 1786 and was buried in the old West Highland churchyard there. Her grave was in 1920 removed to the Greenock Cemetery in Inverkip Road where the original grave stands alongside a later memorial.

At Failford, in a small enclosure on the north side of the main road, can be seen a sandstone column topped by a ball finial. This was erected in May 1921 by the Burns Federation with funds provided by Messrs. Harland and Wolff (shipbuilders in Greenock) to commemorate the spot where Burns and Mary parted. It bears the inscription:

> *Near this spot Robert Burns and Highland Mary took their last farewell, 14th May 1786. 1759-1796.*
> *That sacred hour can I forget,*
> *Can I forget the hallowed grove,*
> *Where by the winding Ayr we met,*
> *To live one day of parting love.*

The River Ayr Way leaves the proximity of the roadside again below Failford, heading through a deep gorge that is richly wooded. At the north end of the gorge, at the west end of Failford, can be seen a deep pool in the wood. This is the remains of an old sandstone quarry. A walker on the path fails to see this, for the Way keeps close to the river side immediately west of the Fail Bridge and follows a route into the Ayr Gorge woodland reserve.

This reserve extends to one hundred acres, operated by the Scottish Wildlife Trust. Known as the Ayr Gorge Woodland, the reserve comprises of Coilsholm Wood and other woods on the opposite side of the river. The woods are a beautifully quiet location on the banks of the river, carefully managed to promote natural wildlife. There have been woods here for centuries, the gorge being so remote and difficult of access that they have not been felled. From the bridge across the mouth of the Fail, a path heads down alongside the river into the reserve. The River Ayr has carved a route through the red sandstone, and to either side grow fine specimens of trees, mainly sessile oak and birch. Under the larger trees grow holly, rowan and hazel trees. Over the years the trust has removed species that are not native to Scotland.

Within the reserve one can often see a wide selection of birds, such as kingfishers, grey wagtails, goosanders, dippers, spotted flycatchers and greater spotted woodpeckers. Otters, roe deer, foxes, badgers and bats can also be seen, and in the spring the floor of the wood is home to a variety of flowers, in particular bluebells. Among the rare plants to be seen are cow-wheat, wood fescue and Dutch rush. Some areas have coverings of heather and blaeberry, and parts of the woodland floor are covered in wood sorrel and wood anemone.

From entering the reserve at Failford, the path crosses the small stream that drains from Coilsholm fields and climbs some steps up to the top of the bank. It then turns south and heads high above the riverbank through the wildlife reserve. At one point a large smooth sandstone wall can be seen at right angles to the river, the remains of a small sandstone quarry. Other paths allow day visitors to make figure of eight and other looped walks in the woods. The path joins an old carriage drive that was created through the woods hereabouts around 1850-60 by the Earl of Eglinton. This left the policies of Montgomerie Castle (also known as Coilsfield House) at a gatehouse that stood just west of the Fancy Bridge over the railway. It probably only went as far as a small field that lay alongside the river, perhaps used for picnics from the big house. This field has long-since overgrown with trees.

Beyond the shelter by the riverside the path splits. The left hand (nearest the river) is a dead-end route now, but it is certainly worth following it into the cul-de-sac. At its end, from a wooden platform, can be seen steps carved from the natural sandstone cliff. This spot is known as Peden's Cove, or cave, although there is no cavern there. It is named after Rev Alexander Peden, the famous Covenanter. He is known to have come here to deliver a sermon to his congregation who were seated on the opposite side of the river, at Windiegoat Wood. The steps gave access to the point where Peden is thought to have preached from, known as Peden's Pulpit. It is said that Peden delivered his last sermon here, and local tradition maintained that it produced an immense impact on the congregation. According to Rev David Ritchie, writing in the *New Statistical Account*, 'many of Peden's admiring hearers used to assemble before the pulpit with their loaded firelocks in their hands.' Peden is not the only Covenanting

Peden's Cove

minister to have preached here. According to the Privy Council records of 1676, they were informed of 'a numerous conventicle lately held at Coilum Wood, in the Laird of Coilfield's lands, at which John Welch, a declared traitor, preached.'

Although the steps at Peden's Cove can be climbed to the pulpit, beyond it is rather airy and dangerous. It is advisable to follow the path back from the viewing platform to the split in the pathway and take the right-hand, or higher route. The path climbs gradually up the slopes to a point on the edge of the wood, next to a summer seat at two massive beech trees. From here the first loop of the reserve's figure of eight walk can be followed more directly back to Failford.

Walkers following the River Ayr Way will continue across the small wooden bridge and into Coilsholm Wood. Within this can be seen many oak trees, and it is worth noting that they often grow in clumps of two or three. This came about due to the original ancient oaks being cut down during the First World War for timber. The stumps that were left threw up shoots which were left to grow unchecked, resulting in tall but thin trees. Along the river one can often see fishermen, for the angling here is the preserve of Tarbolton and Failford Angling Club.

The path continues through the woods of oak, elm, ash and other species before dropping down to the riverside once more. A number of massive beech trees and other varieties grow here, as well as thin spindly trees on ground where once pine trees had been planted. At the western end of the wood another set of steps brings one to the top of the banking, and the southern limit of the wildlife trust's reserve. The second loop of the figure of eight makes its return here, heading north alongside the edge of the wood.

The path now follows the edge of the fields of Clune farm, above the river, and gradually drops down towards the riverside, opposite Stairhill Wood. In spring primroses can be seen growing among the hedges. Around the riverside here, although there appear to be no remains of the building, stood Clune Mill. A short length of watercourse may be a fragment of the mill lade. It was a difficult mill to reach by road, and most of the corn was conveyed there on crooksaddles. The mill had only one pair of stones and the meal produced was sifted by hand. At one time the miller was Andrew Tannock, who died on 25 March 1785 aged 60 years – he is buried in Tarbolton kirkyard.

The path now passes through more open countryside as it makes its way towards Daldorch farm. The River Ayr is followed closely from Clune Mill to Milton. On the southern side of the river is the North Bank, a steep deciduous wood that shelters Daldorch, giving it the name 'dark holm', in Gaelic.

The Way circles Daldorch holm and enters Wellflat (sometimes spelled Wolflet) Bank, a small broadleaf wood on the north side of the river. This wood is owned by the Forestry Commission, despite its small size. There is a considerable amount of giant hogweed growing alongside the river here. Introduced as an ornamental plant in some large gardens, it has become a serious problem due to it spreading along the riverbanks. The sap from the stems is poisonous and can burn the skin. Looking south across the wide river one can see the large dwelling of Stair House Farm, a tight collection of buildings, one an old building with corbie-stepped gables. Just beyond, the ancient fortified house of Stair House comes into view, virtually a small castle. And just behind Stair House can be seen Stair Parish Church.

The path wanders through the wood and heads to the community of Milton, on the north side of Stair Bridge. Crossing the river is a weir, and the former sluice gate and lade survive at the west, bridged by the pathway. From the dam the path heads west to the B730 road at Milton.

One of the cottages on the east side of the road, backing on to the weir, was Stair Bridge Toll Cottage.

Although the River Ayr Way keeps to the north side of the

Stair Bridge

Stair Inn

river at Stair, it is worthwhile crossing the old bridge to explore
the kirk and area around the inn.

Stair Bridge is one of the oldest and finest bridges across the
River Ayr. It is crossed by the B730, which was laid out as a road
to link Irvine with Dalmellington, but the southern part, across
the high moorlands south of Rankinston, has degenerated from
being a public road to being little more than a minor path, often
lost on the ground. The bridge was erected in 1745. It has three
masonry arches on triangular cutwaters. Within eleven years the
foundations were noted as being weak, and old milestones from
the county were used in the river bed to help protect the pier
footings.

On the south side of Stair Bridge is the little community of
Stair itself. Here is the Stair Inn, a very attractive country inn,
serving food and offering accommodation. The inn probably dates
from around 1700, but it has been extended a number of times
over the years. In the first decades of the nineteenth century,
when the parish church at Stair was being restored, church
services were held at the inn instead. The landlord was in the habit
of offering everyone a drink, and it was noted that attendance on
a Sunday was never better than at that time.

Stair Church itself is an attractive small building, located
down a lane from the inn, within its old kirkyard. The church
building dates from 1864, being opened on 27 December, and was
designed by William Alexander. Gothic in style, it can seat 400
worshippers, and has a rose window made by Stephen Adam of
Glasgow. The church replaced an older building that was

Stair House

described as being rather like a barn, distinguished only by a small belfry. Stair parish was created in 1669 by disjoining a large tract of Ochiltree parish and some adjoining lands, covering 5301 acres in total. It was said that this was only done to please the future 1st Viscount of Stair, who found it troublesome to travel the 5½ miles to Ochiltree church.

Stair kirkyard has a few interesting gravestones within it. Buried here is Mrs Catherine Stewart (d. 1818), a friend of Robert Burns. The poet sent her a number of verses in September 1786 which are now preserved in the Burns Cottage museum. These are known as the Stair Manuscript. Another collection, the Afton Manuscript, was also prepared for Mrs Stewart, and is also at Alloway. Also interred here is James Andrew, miller at Barskimming, who vied with Burns over the love of Kate Kemp. There is also a modern headstone commemorating Robert Cameron Corbett (1940-99), youngest son of the 2nd Lord Rowallan. Corbett lived latterly at Stair House, which can be seen across the field from the church to the north. He has an amusing epitaph noting that he lies here, 'prostrate as usual'.

Stair House is a rather fine old Scots tower house, dating from the seventeenth century, though parts of it may predate this. The main block is three storeys in height, plus an attic, and wings form it into an L plan. At one corner is a fine narrow round tower, complete with sealed shot-holes and three string courses. At the opposite end of the garden front is a lower, but wider, drum tower. A tower of a similar diameter, but three storeys in height is located at the north-east end of the house. The main entrance is located in the re-entrant angle. The ground floor has a vaulted storeroom, indicative of its age. There are three public rooms and six bedrooms. Stair was for many years the home of the Earls of Stair, who have the surname Dalrymple, taken from another Ayrshire village.

The Dalrymple of Stair family played an important part in Scotland's history. William de Dalrymple inherited the lands of Stair through his wife in 1429, founding the family. The Dalrymples were raised to the peerage as Viscounts of Stair in 1690 and as Earls of Stair in 1703. James Dalrymple (1619-95) was born at Dinmurchie in the parish of Barr and was educated at Mauchline and Glasgow University, where he became Professor of Logic in 1641. He was instrumental in getting Charles II restored to the crown and was awarded a baronetcy in 1664. He wrote the *Institutions of the Law of Scotland* in 1681, which is better known as the 'Stair Institutions'. This was an important contribution to the formalising of Scots Law and is still referred to at present. It was he who was created Viscount Stair. His son, John Dalrymple (1648-1707), 1st Earl of Stair, whilst Master of Stair, persuaded William III to sign the document that resulted in the Massacre of Glencoe in 1692, when the Campbells infamously routed the MacDonalds of Glencoe. Three other sons were all awarded baronetcies.

John Dalrymple (1673-1747), 2nd Earl of Stair, was a Field Marshal and ambassador to several continental countries. He was active at the Battle of Dettingen in 1743 and on his return planted some woodland around Stair House in the shape of the battle formation. Most of these trees have long-since been felled, but an old beech tree near to the church is thought to represent the General, and is so named. In the late seventeenth century a tragic accident occurred at Stair House when the young Field Marshal Stair was playing with a gun and accidentally shot his elder brother, heir of the 1st Earl, resulting in him becoming the next earl in turn. This is thought to have taken place in a room on the ground floor of the house, long locked up. Some accounts, however, place this accident at Carsecreugh House in Wigtownshire.

The Dalrymples sold Stair for a time, and during the ownership of Catherine Stewart the house was visited by Robert Burns. Mrs Stewart heard the poet singing and reciting poems in the kitchen, for the benefit of the servants. She invited him up to the drawing room to entertain, starting a long friendship. Mrs Stewart sold Stair House in 1796. The Dalrymples repurchased Stair around 1826.

2nd Earl of Stair

The Dalrymple family also owned other estates in Scotland, such as Newliston near Kirkliston in West Lothian and Oxenfoord Castle near Dalkeith in Midlothian, which they used when in Edinburgh, and also Lochinch Castle, near Stranraer, which is their current seat. Stair House was the smallest of these, and in 1930 Lord Stair had the house restored under the direction of the architect, James Carrick of Ayr. For a number of years Stair was leased out by the family, for many years to the Lockharts, but it has in recent years been sold to Colonel Michael Bullen. There were three old mills at Stair – a corn mill, lint mill and mill for cleaning grass seed. One of these operated for a short time as a factory manufacturing curling stones. A woollen mill was opened on New Year's Day in 1830 by James Heron of Dalmore and this operated until 1908. Another mill is adorned by a carving of a sheaf of corn, and bears the legend W Heron 1821. The seed mill was operated by John Lennox in the seventeenth century. He was a noted Covenanter and was shot on his own doorstep by dragoons. Where he was buried is not known.

At Milton is an old mill building where the famous Tam o' Shanter hone and Water of Ayr stone are made. These naturally occurring and very fine sharpening stones are found in the ground in the locality, and are cut and shaped in the works. The stone has been worked on the Dalmore estate since 1789. At one time the stone was quarried, but latterly it was mined. Remains of the mines can be seen at Stair Wood and Dalmore, the latter being the most recently operated. The Water of Ayr and Tam o' Shanter Hone Works Limited company was founded on 2 October 1900 and is still in existence.

The Milton Mill was powered by water from the dam across

the River Ayr, located a few hundred yards upstream from Stair Bridge. An attempt to raise the dam around 1893 failed, when the river flooded, destroying most of the new work. Instead a concrete dam was erected, and this was faced with stone. This dam cost over £1000 to build, the workmen being paid four shillings per day for ten hours work, and the cement cost less than £2 per ton.

Also produced at Milton during the Second World War was grey paint, used for painting battleships. Thousands, if not millions of gallons of paint were made here and adorned ships that travelled the world.

Dalmore estate was at one time home of the Heron family but was sold to the Montgomeries in 1876. The old mansion house that was erected 1880-81 in a castellated style stands in ruins among the woods, and the former stable block is now converted into cottages. The house may have been designed by the Kilmarnock architect, Robert Ingram. Dalmore House was destroyed in a fire in April 1969.

4. STAIR to AUCHINCRUIVE

The River Ayr Way makes its way up through the community of Milton, heading north along the B730. Just as the road swings to the right, the Way takes left, into the fields of Enterkine, and onto the Enterkine Holm, a large flat floodplain bounded to the north by the wooded Holm Bank. At the top of the Holm Bank, on the crest of a low hill, is an ancient earthen mound, perhaps a Bronze Age burial cairn or barrow. It measures around 25 feet in diameter and rises approximately four feet high. Around it is a ditch approximately five feet wide, though today it is only eight inches deep, having silted up over the years. There may be a low external bank beyond the ditch to the south.

A low hill in this vicinity is known as the Payment Hill. It gets its name from a battle that is claimed to have been fought here between the Danes and Scots, at some unknown point in history. The Danes are supposed to have landed at Ayr and fought their way inland, pushing the Scots back. When reinforcements arrived, the Scots were victorious in battle here, routing the Danes, or Vikings as they may have been, and taking their payment. During subsequent ploughing, various spearheads were found. The mound on Holm Bank may have been some form of burial associated with the battle.

The path keeps to the foot of the Holm Bank, before striking south towards the riverside at the ruins of Enterkineholm farm. This was a typical U-shaped courtyard farmstead with a circular horse gin house to the north. Little of the farm buildings remain, though the ruins of the gable can be seen from the path. On the south side of the river, between Dalmore and Laigh Dalmore, is the old whetstone mine, occupying the site of Dalmore whetstone quarry.

At Enterkineholm was an old ford across the river, leading to Laigh Dalmore. The path follows an old track between the fields and the river west from here. This narrow strip of uncultivated ground is home to many interesting wild flowers and large trees.

At the top of the western end of Holm Bank stands Enterkine House, a modern country house of 1939 built to plans of John Fairweather & Sons of Glasgow. The house is now a rather fine restaurant and hotel, serving the best of food, located within a 310 acre estate. The present house replaced an old mansion of the late eighteenth century, demolished due to a serious outbreak of dry rot. Enterkine is an ancient estate, owned by the Cunninghame family since the mid seventeenth century.

At the time of Robert Burns it was the home of William Cunninghame (son in law of Mrs Stewart of Stair), grandson of the previous owner. It was he who organised The Fete Champetre that is referred to by Burns in his song of that title. This was to mark Cunninghame's coming of age, as well as to try to influence local nobility into electing him as MP for Ayrshire. The fete took place somewhere on the holm below Enterkine in the summer of 1788, though its exact location has never been confirmed – some think that it was on the flat holm between Annbank House (Cunninghame's other inheritance) and Privick Mill. The event lasted for three days and was brought to an abrupt end when a thunderstorm erupted from the skies. In Burns' song he criticises the use of wine and coin in trying to buy votes:

> *Ane gi'es them coin, ane gi'es them wine,*
> *Anither gi'es them clatter;*
> *Annbank, wha guess'd the ladies' taste,*
> *He gi'es a Fete Champetre.*

Cunninghame didn't stand for parliament after all.

Enterkine Holm disappears where the wooded bank runs down to the riverside. The path keeps close to the bottom of the bank, passing through a section of woodland. Above, on the top of the bank, is the old walled garden of Enterkine. In the woods grow primroses, sorrel and giant hogweed.

On the opposite side of the river, on a small holm at Knockshoggle, stood the lost village of Knockshoggle Holm. In 1841 it had a population of 109. At a later date there were only eight cottages remaining there, of which some were thatched. Little is apparent now that at one time there was a small community here, other than a few low ruins of walls. Clay-slates, or Water of Ayr stones, were also to be found here and were worked for a time, but the trade died when the works at Stair took off. Ducks can often be seen in the river along the last stretch.

The path continues alongside the river and soon passes below the Enterkine Viaduct. This bridge was erected in 1872 as part of the Ayr to Cumnock line and has fourteen stone-built piers supporting a shallow-plate steel girder superstructure, about 90 feet above the level of the river. The viaduct carried the railway line from Annbank Station south to join the Cumnock and Edinburgh railway line. Today the line is still used to allow coal from various open cast mines to be transported from the loading station at the former Killoch Colliery onto the main lines.

The Way keeps to the riverside from the viaduct downstream to Gadgirth Bridge, crossing the mouth of Crawfordston Burn. The south bank of the river is wooded, the slopes of Gadgirth Hill being covered with deciduous trees. At one time there were a couple of cottages in the wood there, one known as Gadgirth Cottage.

Gadgirth Bridge carries the B742 across the river, linking Annbank and Mossblown on the north with Coylton to the south. The Bridge is a plate girder structure and was erected in 1909. At either end are cast iron plaques recording *Alexr. Findlay & Co. Limited, Parkneuk Bridge Works, Motherwell, 1909*. This bridge

Gadgirth Bridge

77

replaced an older steel framed bridge that had iron trelliswork sides that had been erected in 1879 by Cameron Richmond. This in turn replaced the old stone-arched bridge, which had a stone inscribed *I was built by Mr John Stell of Gadgirth in 1768*. Rev John Steele was the minister of Stair from 1735 until 1804. He married the Chalmers heiress and inherited Gadgirth estate from her family. He remained minister of Stair for 69 years, dying in 1804 aged 93.

On the southern side of the bridge is Gadgirth Holm, a fine terrace of cottages erected in 1906. They were built on the site of an older row of thatched cottages, erected by Rev John Steele in 1769 to house mineworkers on the estate. In 1841 there were 50 people living here.

Gadgirth House stood on a promontory above the River Ayr to the south of here. There was an old castle on the site, and Gadgirth is mentioned as an old estate in local history, owned by the Chalmers family. There are claims that both John Knox and Mary Queen of Scots visited Gadgirth, the former dispensing communion and the latter sleeping one night in the old tower. The mansion house that was demolished in 1968 was a simple Georgian block, three floors in height with a large bowed projection. It had been erected in 1808 by Lieutenant Colonel Joseph Burnett (1753-1833). He had intended enlarging the old tower house that formerly stood here, but when he commenced building works discovered that the walls, despite being six feet thick in places, were so rotten that they were unsafe. In 1949 the house became a children's home run by the county council but it became too costly to run and was closed in 1968, the house being demolished shortly thereafter. Today a modern wooden-built house occupies the site.

On the low hill to the south of Gadgirth Bridge stands a squat obelisk, originally an eye-catcher when viewed from Gadgirth House. The obelisk rises above Gadgirth Mains, a delightful former stable courtyard with a number of arched windows.

Along the B742 from Gadgirth Bridge, at Crawfordston, was the lost village of Burnbrae, which originally comprised of nineteen houses in three rows. The houses, which were mainly thatched, were demolished in 1928. They were occupied by miners who worked in a number of small pits that littered the district. At Burnbrae there was also a small school, known as Weston School.

The River Ayr Way keeps to the north side of the river, heading towards the woods below Annbank. A number of paths can be followed up through the woods to the village, which sits on top of the hill. The path gradually rises through the woods and around a sharp bend in the river, below Annbank. Just short of the bend a large rounded boulder can be seen in the centre of the river.

Annbank is a fairly modern community, established as a mining village by George Taylor & Co., the local mine owners, around 1860. The Ordnance Survey map of that date shows the site of the village as open fields. Single-storey cottages lined Weston Avenue, but most of these old miners' rows have been demolished and replaced by council housing of the 1930s, so that the village appears to have little appearance of antiquity. There is one local shop (Braefoot Stores) and a post office here. There is also a public house (Tap o' the Brae), Annbank United's football ground (New Pebble Park) and a bowling club.

In the small square in the middle of Weston Avenue is a white granite monument commemorating James Brown MP (1862-1939), who lived in the village, latterly at 51 Weston Avenue. Brown was born in Whitletts, the son of a miner, and developed his interest in trade unions. He became secretary of the Ayrshire Miners' Union as well as the Scottish Miners National Union. He first stood for parliament in 1910, but was beaten. In 1918 he was elected as the first Labour MP for South Ayrshire, remaining until 1931. He held the seat again from 1935 until his death in 1939, aged 76. He was on three occasions appointed Lord High Commissioner to the General Assembly of the Church of Scotland, and he had various honours bestowed on him. The memorial was unveiled in 1954.

The River Ayr Way makes its way along an old pathway in the grounds of what was Annbank House. The site of this house is located on a knoll that drops steeply to the river. In the woods (known here as Broad Wood) can be seen old yew trees, as well as holly and rhododendron bushes. Unfortunately there is also a lot of litter, items being dumped here from the village above. On the pathway below the site of the house is a summer seat with fine views upstream to Gadgirth Bridge and Holm.

Annbank House was latterly owned by the local coalmasters, the Clarke family. The house was probably originally a farmhouse, named Privick, but various extensions resulted in it becoming a sizeable property. It received its name when Lady Ann Montgomery married the laird and he renamed the estate in her honour. As a result the village of Annbank also received its name. Annbank House was long owned by the Cunninghames of Enterkine, and was probably their dower house before it became associated with mine owners. It was demolished in the 1970s.

Today a small picnic area, accessed from Dunlop Avenue in Annbank, occupies part of the site of the house.

The River Ayr Way leaves the picnic area at the site of Annbank House and takes a detour into Annbank village itself. It soon joins Dunlop Avenue, which is followed to the main road (B744) at Weston Avenue. The route is then followed south-westwards along Braeside to Mill Road, which strikes south from the village. This road is followed down towards an old nursery, the tall brick tower of the hothouse chimney still rising high. It had to be extended upwards at one time when the residents of Whitehill Crescent and Braeside in Annbank complained that the smoke was hitting their homes. The track terminates at Privick Mill, a collection of old sandstone buildings including a large house, which is located at the side of the river. The Way misses the house by striking across a field, rejoining the River Ayr just south of the mill.

Privick Mill was in fact two mills side by side – a flour mill and an oatmeal mill, though the 1860 Ordnance Survey map notes that it was a corn mill. One of the old mill buildings has a rough date of 1791 carved onto a door lintel. Each mill had a waterwheel around fifteen feet in diameter, by four feet wide. They required around three thousand cubic feet of water per minute to operate a full load. Around 1860 a kiln for drying wheat was added alongside the mill. The mill closed just before the Second World War.

Privick Mill

Writing in *Rambles on the Banks of Ayr* in 1884, 'Rab the Rambler' gives a fairly detailed description of the mill at that time:

But as I remember it first, the mill was a long, low, narrow building, with a thatch roof. It stood with its gable end to the water. The kiln-head was made of perforated tiles, and beside it was a loft for storing the undried corn. Below this loft was a barley mill, driven by a water wheel of its own, and outside in a shed were a pair of grindstones, where in summer, James Brown, of Ochiltree, ground his reaping hooks, for that was before the days of reaping machines. But let me describe the mill to you. The water wheel is just outside the gable; it is made entirely of wood; the axle is an oak tree hooped with iron, and with iron gudgeons in the ends, which run in whinstone bushes. The arms of the wheel are oak planks, and the rim is also of oak, with oak starts and alder floats. Inside the mill is the pit wheel, also of oak; the bridge tree, oak too. Only the millstone spindle and pinion are iron, and the foot of the spindle runs in a stone footstep, the stones set on a platform about six feet high across the end of the mill. There are two pairs. One pair, about five feet in diameter, are driven direct from the pit wheel. These are for shelling oats and milling oatmeal. The other pair sit in the corner; they are about four feet in diameter, and are used for mashlam, beans, etc.

He also noted that the millstones were brought from a notable quarry at Kaimshill, near West Kilbride, which is around 25 miles distant.

The detour into Annbank taken by the Way is to allow the occupiers of the mill house some privacy. A path does drop from the site of Annbank House down towards the end of the old weir, with two sluices that allowed some of the water into a lade to the disused mill. An archway from where the water from the river passed through can still be seen on part of the weir that survives. The lade remains water-filled for much of its way. The pathway used by locals follows the narrow strip of ground between it and the river. A number of large oak and beech trees grow here, the wood floor being carpeted with wood anemone and other wild flowers.

On the opposite side of the river one can see the high sandstone wall that surrounds the old walled garden of Gadgirth House. Today the gardens have some log cabins within them, rented out to holidaymakers. A number of fishing platforms can be seen at Gadgirth, and they become ever more popular from here downstream.

The Way rejoins the riverside immediately to the south of Privick Mill. Just to the south of the old mill is an old freestone quarry, the low vertical rock visible across the field. This was no doubt used to build the mill buildings.

From Privick Mill the Way keeps to the riverside, though the path keeps to the top of a steep drop into the river. Here and there small steps lead down to spots for fishing, often with shelters or summer seats alongside. A couple of gates are passed through at a small wood, where the Way climbs over a rock promontory. This constriction forces the river through between the rocks, creating a large deep pool, known as the Auld Ha' Weel, on the downstream side. It is claimed that this pool is the deepest in the whole River Ayr, and is 55 feet in depth. The swirling waters create a whirlpool, which in storms has been known to drag down tree trunks that have been knocked into the river.

On the top of the high rock on the south bank can be found the remnants of the Old Ha', perched on a promontory, where the river has to make a few sharp turns due to the natural formation of the land. Below this promontory are a few islands in the river, one of which is perhaps the largest in the whole length of the river. Being inaccessible it is richly wooded. A lesser island has dozens of tree trunks at the top of it, caught here when they were being washed downstream.

The Old Ha' was the original Gadgirth Castle, superseded by a later castle where Gadgirth House latterly stood. The Old Ha' was erected on a whinstone rock, projecting into the river course, which protects it on two sides. The other two sides were at one time protected from attack by a fosse, or ditch, which measures about 30 feet across and is over three feet deep.

Today only one stretch of masonry wall about eighteen feet in length and eleven feet high survives, built against a rock outcrop, and another part defining a corner. According to John Paterson in *The History of Ayrshire*, the ditch was crossed by a drawbridge. The area covered by the building was around 28 feet by 19 feet.

The Old Ha' was a Chalmers seat, that family having held Gadgirth since around 1100, according to a charter issued by King James VI. During the reign of William the Lion (1165-1214), the Gadgirth lands were owned by Reginaldus de Camera, or Chalmers, as the name became.

The River Ayr Way keeps to the riverside. On the south bank of the river is the Oldhall Wood, and at the turn below the large island is a fisherman's shelter and summer seats. The deep pool at the foot of the island is known as Berbeth Weel. The path keeps to the bottom of a steep embankment to the south of Woodhill, a ruined farmhouse. For part of the way it has been built up by fishermen to create a riverside path, at one stretch utilising flat beds of rock. More fishing huts and seats are passed as the path follows the side of the river. The countryside opens out once more, a large floodplain on the north side of the river being known as Lowrie's Holm.

Soon the mouth of the Water of Coyle is reached, its confluence in the Ayr being at a deep pool, known as the Mill Weel. At one time a mill existed hereabouts, but it has been demolished for centuries. The Water of Coyle drains much of the countryside to the south and is the last major tributary of the River Ayr to join it.

Below the mouth of the Coyle, where the opposite side of the river is occupied by the Barclach Wood, is a massive black-coloured rock in the middle of the river. The path keeps to the riverside, passing below the wood below the ruins of Monkhead cottage and arriving at the B744 at Tarholm Bridge.

Somewhere between the mouth of the Coyle and Tarholm Bridge, on the farm of Barclach, or Barclaugh, four prehistoric stone coffins, or sarcophagi, were discovered in the nineteenth century. The exact location where these were unearthed or where they are today is unknown.

Tarholm Bridge is quite an unusual structure. It has three sandstone piers and two stone abutments, over which is a concrete deck. The sides of the bridge comprise cast concrete balustrades. Some of these have become damaged, revealing the iron wire down the centre. This is the third bridge to occupy this spot.

Tarholm was a small village comprising two rows of cottages, located back from the road in the large meander of the river. The cottages were thatched and were entitled the Big and Wee rows. The name Tarholm derives from the story that Archibald Cochrane, 9th Earl of Dundonald, established a tar distilling plant here, using locally mined coal. The former distillery was a large barn-like building. The site of the Wee Row is now occupied by Stanalane cottage, a modern brick building with red tiled roof. The Big Row is occupied by Riverslea cottage and Tarholm Nursery. Plant sales take place here in season.

The Way crosses Tarholm Bridge and then makes its way down the left bank of the river. The B744 turns sharply to the left, heading south to the Belston Holdings at the A70. The path keeps to the side of the river, passing through a wooded bank. Here can be seen sorrel and primroses in season. The deep pool at the bend of the river is known as the Craighall Weel.

The landscape around Annbank and Auchincruive is quite unusual, for it is formed of a number of small hills. Some of these have names, and many are topped by round or other shaped woods, known in Ayrshire as 'mounts'.

On the hillside above stood a village known as Craighall, the houses arranged around a square. There were twenty houses that formed a U-shaped courtyard, the north side being separate from the other houses. It is claimed that the houses were at one time stables before being converted into miners' homes. In 1841 the population was around 100. To the west is Barrackhall, where more cottages were located. This place is supposed to have been a barracks at one time, and the stables would have been connected with them. The old cottages have gone, demolished around 1933, and today only a couple of houses remain at the site of this lost village.

For the next couple of miles the river flows generally northwards, again following a deep gorge that is richly wooded. This was at one time part of Auchincruive estate, the largest estate in this locality. The path follows the river bank at the foot of the steep Craighall Bank, before leaving the wood and entering an open field. This was at one time part of the larger wood. On the opposite bank of the river can be seen Riverslea house with the tennis court in the grounds. At the opposite end of the field the path enters Craighall Wood, another large mixed wood by the riverside. The path gradually climbs above the level of the water.

Just over half a mile downstream from Tarholm Bridge, where the west side of the river rises steeply from the waterside, can be seen the rock outcrop known as Wallace's Seat. This is traditionally supposed to have been a spot where William Wallace, Scotland's great freedom fighter, hid from the English foe in the thirteenth century. The seat occupies a high rock outcrop, from where it is a vertical drop down to the river. A number of large trees grow here, and a fence stops visitors from falling over the edge. A wooden bench has been placed here, with views over to Annbank area.

From Wallace's Seat the path drops down to the riverside once more, and follows it northwards through Craighall Wood. Around one mile from Tarholm Bridge can be seen the remnants of two stone pillars built to support an old wagon way bridge that crossed the river here. This part of the wagon way appears to date from just after 1860 and linked the pits of Annbank and Enterkine to Ayr. On the opposite side of the river from the Way, at the foot of the Muir Burn, is the site of the Brockle Quarry.

This spot is popular with walkers from Annbank, and the fishermen have created a shelter and stone-built wharf by the riverside.

The Brockle Quarry is where the stone used for the famous sculptures of Tam o' Shanter and Souter Johnnie was dug. These statues were executed by James Thom (1799-1850) and depict the two men sitting in the inn drinking ale, prior to Tam's epic journey in which he was pursued by the witches from Alloway Auld Kirk. The statues can be seen in a shelter within the garden of Souter Johnnie's Cottage at Kirkoswald, which is preserved by the National Trust for Scotland.

A few hundred yards downstream from the site of the bridge the river takes a large bend, circling anti clockwise around a spot known as the Pheasant Nook. On the opposite bank of the river the land rises steeply back up to the village of Annbank, just half a mile away, the hill on which it stands being virtually surrounded by a great sweep of the river.

The River Ayr swings almost one hundred and eighty degrees around the Sheep Park and heads westwards. The Way leaves the river side for a spell, making its way through the Pheasant Nook wood. Higher up to the left is the Coronation Wood. The woods hereabouts comprise mainly of beech, oak, Japanese larch and Scots pine. This part of the walk follows the old wagon way that crossed the lost bridge. It is located on top of a low embankment. The furthest point of the river is bypassed for a spell, before the path returns closer to it. At one point a large pipe crosses the river.

The Way reaches a junction of paths. The official route keeps to the riverside and takes the route to the right. The path to the left, climbing up a track through the Cutting Wood, can be used as a slight shortcut.

The path leaves the wood and enters an open field known as 'Three Green Knights Park'. This is supposed to get its name from the three mounds that are visible in the field. Here fine views can be had westward, encompassing Auchincruive House and its gardens. The path reaches a public road at The Knowe cottage, near to Oswald's Bridge, a fine stone bridge across the river.

The Cutting referred to in 'Cutting Wood' is actually the railway cutting of an early wagon system that was used to transport coal from small mines hereabouts to Ayr. In 1857 the tramway reached Oswald's Bridge, and soon after it was continued onto the land beyond, where existed the Peelhill pits. The Ordnance Survey map of 1860 indicates two coal pits hereabouts, one near to the riverside, just north of Oswald's Bridge (Peelhill No. 1), and the other by the side of the track that passes between Mount Loudoun and Mount Stair (Peelhill No. 2). These pits seem to have closed by 1869.

On the west side of Oswald's Bridge, on the south side of the public road, stood the Holm Pit, which operated in the 1860s. On the Ordnance Survey map of the time this was the eastern terminus of a tramway to Ayr. Today there is no sign of a coal mine having existed here.

The fields on Peel Hill were at one time home to a herd of wild white cattle. These cows and bulls were similar to the famous Cadzow cattle that lived near to Chatelherault in Lanarkshire, or the Chillingham wild cows in Northumberland. The wild herd had belonged to the Cathcarts from time immemorial but it was removed in 1784 by Richard Oswald as he found them to be 'useless and troublesome'.

Oswald's bridge was erected in 1826, which date appeared on the parapet. It has a large central arch and two smaller side or relief arches. The cut-waters are carried up vertically to provide pedestrian refuges part-way across the bridge. An older bridge occupied the same site, probably erected around 1770 when the mansion was being rebuilt and the grounds improved. At the west end of the bridge, where the drive leads north to Auchincruive

Oswald's Bridge

House, stood the Bridge
Lodge, a gatehouse for the
estate, but this has long-
since been demolished.

The area around the
bridge is a popular place
for spotting wildlife, which
includes dippers, ducks
and herons.

In the wood to the
south east of the bridge is
a large stone cairn, erected
in September 1929 by the
Burns Federation to
commemorate two of
Ayrshire's heroes – Robert
Burns and William

Wallace Cairn, Leglen

Wallace. Ground for the cairn was gifted by John M. Hannah of
Girvan Mains and the cost of construction was defrayed by Rev J.
C. Higgins, minister of Tarbolton. The cairn was built to
commemorate the time when the young Robert Burns walked to
Auchincruive and heard the stories of William Wallace and his
fight for Scottish freedom. The cairn bears the inscription:

> *Wallace and Burns*
> *O never, never, Scotia's realm desert,*
> *But still the patriot and the bard,*
> *In bright succession raise her ornament and guard.*
>
> *Syne to the Leglen Wood, when it was late*
> *To make a silent and safe retreat.*

The quotes are taken from Blind Harry's epic poem, *The Life
of Sir William Wallace*, and the second one refers to the time when
Wallace made his escape from Ayr to the woods and gorges of
Auchencruive for safety. A number of references to the
Auchincruive area can be found in *The Wallace*:

> *Then to Laigland wood, when it grew late,*
> *To make a silent and a soft retreat.*
> *Some little time thereafter did repair*
> *Unto the pleasant ancient town of Ayr;*
> *Close by the wood, did there dismount his horse,*
> *Then on his feet, walk'd gravely to the cross.*

After Wallace had killed some Englishmen in Ayr, he...

> *Made his escape, and then did mount his horse:*
> *To Laiglands he fled, his time he well did use,*
> *And left the blades all sleeping in their shoes.*
> *Him foot and horse pursue to overtake,*
> *But the thick trees his refuge he did make.*
> *Provisions came to him from Ochter house,*
> *And ev'ry thing that was fit for his own use.*

The reference to Ochter house is a variant of Auchencruive.
On another occasion Wallace killed the Buckler player in Ayr, and
again 'rode for better safety to the Laigland wood.'

Auchincruive House is located by the side of the River Ayr,
800 yards north of the bridge, on the west bank. The house was
erected in 1767 to plans by Robert Adam, and it has been
extended in an Adam style. It was James Murray who
commissioned Adam, but the house was probably either
unfinished, or not started when he sold the estate on. When it was
built the house had been altered somewhat from Adam's plans.
Later wings and alterations were made to create the fine mansion
as it stands today.

Internally Auchincruive House still retains a number of fine
Adam rooms. Adam's own drawings prove that the ceilings of
some of the public rooms are to his design. The entrance hall is
the apartment furnished most like his original plans. The Dining
Room has another Adam ceiling, and the Music Room has an
Adam fireplace.

West of the big house, which is now known as Oswald Hall,
stands Gibbsyard, the former mains farm of the estate. The
courtyard is an impressive building, erected in 1767. It has a
depressed archway leading under a square tower into a courtyard.

Auchincruive House

The tower boasts a clock and is topped by an unusual convex roof with glass cupola and wind vane.

Auchincruive was anciently a seat of the Wallace family, but in 1380 it passed to the Cathcarts of Sundrum Castle. The Cathcarts sold it to James Murray of Cally in 1758. He retained the estate for only a short period, before selling it on to Richard Oswald in 1764.

Richard Oswald (1705-84) was a wealthy merchant who had made his fortune in London as an importer of tobacco and other goods. He was also involved in the slave trade, in 1748 being a partner in a firm established in Sierra Leone for dealing in African slaves. He acquired extensive estates in North America through marriage and from the crown. He was heavily involved in the American War of Independence where he was noted for his negotiating skills. He was a signatory in the preliminary treaty of 30 November 1782, and gained the nickname, 'Richard the Peacemaker'. In Florida his former plantation of Mount Oswald is now the Tomoko State Park, where a memorial was erected in his memory, and an island in the Florida Keys was named after him. He died at Auchincruive and was buried in the kirkyard at St Quivox.

In 1927 John M. Hannah of Girvan Mains gifted the estate of Auchincruive to the West of Scotland Agricultural College, which at that time was based in Kilmarnock. Auchincruive allowed the college to expand, and numerous buildings were erected for

Gibbsyard

college purposes. In 1990 the college merged with others in Edinburgh and Aberdeen to become part of the Scottish Agricultural College.

The grounds of Auchincruive are open to the public and there are a number of interesting walks through the woods. There is a small pets' cemetery near to Auchincruive house, where stones commemorate two dogs and a squirrel named Chummel. Also near the house are two ice-houses, one of which was restored in 1983.

The gardens of Auchincruive are worth making a detour to visit. The most spectacular is the Hanging Garden, thought to have been created in the 1830s or 40s by Richard Alexander Oswald (1771-1841) as a work-creation project for unemployed miners. The stone terraces are 400 feet long and rise up to 30 feet in height. In recent years the Friends of Auchincruive (established 1985) have been active in promoting the grounds.

On the north side of the river, a few hundred yards north-east of Auchincruive House, stood Milnholm Mill, but this seems to have been demolished early in the nineteenth century, if not before. The mill dam only went half way across the river, a fairly unusual occurrence, although the dam at Milton, north of Stair, was formerly like this. The dam made use of a natural whinstone dyke that crossed the river. This spot is known as The Breakers. In 1966, when the River Ayr was severely flooded, it washed away some of the banking to reveal parts of the lade.

Within the policies of Auchincruive can be seen Oswald's Temple, a circular tower built in 1778 to plans by Robert Adam. This was erected as a tea-house, where the family could wander through the pleasure grounds and stop for picnics. The tower, being built on a low hill, was also something of a folly in the parklands, adding to the whole ornamental effect of the estate. The lower floor was latterly converted into a water tank, capable of holding 11,000 gallons of water.

The low hills in the area of land between the western sweep of the River Ayr, between Oswald's Bridge and Tarholm Bridge, all have names associated with the owners of Auchincruive estate. At the north is Mount Loudoun, and south of it is Mount Stair. Further south is Mount Scarburgh, and the fourth in the meander is Mount Mary.

5. Auchincruive to Ayr Harbour

The River Ayr Way crosses Oswald's Bridge and follows the public road westwards towards some college buildings. To the right are iron gates and sandstone pillars, allowing access to Auchincruive House, and the general public can drive up it to a car park from where a number of walks in the grounds of the estate can be made.

The walk keeps to a path on the north side of the road. There is a low dry stone wall at the side, formerly a ha-ha but this is topped with an iron railing and hedges. Views are possible north to Auchincruive House and two other main college buildings.

After passing Craig Rossie cottage, a former mushroom farm on the left, and the college's excavator training centre, the Way then takes a turn to the left, down a private track and along the side of Mount Charles Wood. The track is signposted as a cycle route to Ayr, four and a half miles distant. Mount Charles House is an attractive building, formerly the home of the factor of Auchincruive estate. The house has a fine bow front at one end, and lesser wings are located to the rear.

The track is followed to its end, alongside Mount Charles and Holm woods. These have pine trees as the main crop, with broadleaved trees around the edges. Looking south, over the flat holm fields, are two hillocks topped with trees – these are Mounts Scarburgh and Mary. By the side of the track is an information plaque detailing the crop rotation cycle in the Holm Fields. The track, then path is followed to a minor road at the site of Newbarns cottage.

This minor road was at one time a through route, indeed, where it passes to the west side of Newbarns Wood there is still an old milestone! It proclaims Auchincruive 1 and Ayr 3¾. Another could formerly be seen at Mole Cottage, further along the way, but unfortunately it has been lost.

The River Ayr Way leaves the fields and joins the roadway at the last cottage in the group of smallholdings known as Mainholm Holdings. The public road from here is followed past Aitkenbrae (Number 17 holding), Dove Cottage (Number 14, which is Auchincruive kennels and cattery), Strathayre Nursery, which grows flowers and plants, and Mainholm Nursery. The roadway comes nearer the river at this point, though it is invisible in a hollow at the edge of the field adjoining the road. From Riverside Lodge the Way keeps following the road past Broomhill and Mole Cottage, Cameronsholm and Airlstone Nursery.

The road takes a sharp turn to the right, and the Way follows it past Millview (Number 4 Mainholm Holdings), which is the Scottish Society for the Prevention of Cruelty to Animals' Ayr Animal Welfare Centre. After another sharp turn to the left, the road joins the very busy A77, Ayr by-pass road. The Way heads south along the path at the side of the road to the Overmills Bridge, crossing the River Ayr. From the bridge one can look down to the river and see a set of concrete stepping stones.

The walker may have preferred to cross these stones, though only when the level of the river is low. If desired, the minor road at the first of the sharp bends on Mainholm road should be followed south past two cottages by the riverside. A path then leads down to the stepping stones, which leads one to the southern bank, where at one time the Overmills stood.

The Over Mill, to give it its original name, was in existence from as early as the thirteenth century. It was the property of the Burgh of Ayr for over 300 years. The main building was four storeys in height and had five pairs of stones within it. These were driven by a waterwheel which was twenty feet in diameter by five feet in width, producing around 30-35 horsepower. In 1761 a waulk mill was added to allow the business to expand into fulling, or beating, of cloth. The Over Mill, which was pluralized when the waulk mill was added, was the last working grain mill to operate on the River Ayr. It eventually closed in the 1960s and the buildings were demolished in the spring of 1963. Today there is nothing other than a few masonry walls along the riverside and the remains of the angled weir to indicate the existence of the mill.

From the Overmills Bridge the path turns left and doubles back under the road, preventing the need to cross what is a major route. This bridge was erected in 1963 to take through traffic away from the centre of the town. It is a concrete slab construction, with three low arches on concrete piers and a parapet of railings.

The Way follows paths on the south bank of the river westwards alongside some meadows filled with buttercups. The river turns to the left, and heads southwards for a bit, before heading westwards again. On the low bank stands the large secondary school of Kyle Academy, which has a rugby pitch on the lower field. The school was opened in August 1979.

The path keeps to the riverside, below the academy, and soon crosses a footbridge. On the west side of this bridge is an old three-draw limekiln. This dates from the eighteenth century and was part of the agricultural improvements then being carried out on the Auchincruive estate. On it is a plaque commemorating the creation of the original River Ayr Walk, which went from Ayr town centre upstream as far as Overmills.

The River Ayr Walk was opened to the public on 24 August 1910 by Provost James S. Hunter of Ayr. Previously the walk was jealously guarded by the two estates here – Auchincruive and Craigie, and those following it could be fined. Writing in 1884 following his *Rambles on the Banks of Ayr*, 'Rab the Rambler' noted that much of the land was closed to the public:

> ...and lest the prying rambler should set a sacrilegious foot on the sacred soil which belongs to the Laird of Auchincruive, the wall which bounds the road is topped with broken bottles laid in cement.

Arguments over access to the riverside raged for many years, until in 1910 Richard Alexander Oswald (1841-1921) decided that he would open the route to anyone. From that time on residents of the burgh would walk up one side of the river to the stepping stones and then back down the opposite side. The ground was subject to an entail and he was not able to gift the ground. The plaque also commemorates the fact that some of the grounds were gifted by *A younger son of George Oswald Esq of Auchincruive ... in memory of his elder brother, August 1922*. Again the provost of Ayr, Donald MacDonald, is mentioned, but the two Oswald brothers are not! They were in fact, Richard Alexander and Julian (1860-1943), and the Oswald arms as well as that of the Royal Burgh of Ayr, are on the plaque. The walk was not formally handed over until 30 May 1924, by which time all the legal work had been completed. The plaque was unveiled by Julian's wife, Ethel Oswald. Julian Oswald was elected a Freeman of the Royal Burgh of Ayr in 1924 for his munificent gifts.

On the south side of the river, west of the limekiln, is a small spring issuing water from the rock. This is located right next to the river, and access to it is down steps from the pathway. The spring would be little more than a natural feature but for the connection with Sir William Wallace. According to tradition the freedom fighter was being pursued by English soldiers. He ran this way, and as he jumped from the river his foot made an impression in the rock, still visible. This is known as Wallace's Heel, and the spring is supposed to have run from a crevice ever since. Wallace was successful in his escape, making his way to the Craigie side of the river and into the fastnesses near Auchincruive. Tradition claims that there was a Wallace's Cave on the northern bank of the river near here.

The Way follows the path up towards Holmston Road, but keeps off the main A70 and follows a path through the trees. There are many old oak and beech trees by the path, as well as one or two monkey puzzle trees. On the southern side of the road can be seen the large Holmston Cemetery. Here is buried George Douglas Brown (1869-1902), author of *The House with the Green Shutters,* a strong novel which, when it was published, killed off the kailyard school of writing. Douglas Brown was born in Ochiltree and was educated in Coylton and Ayr. He died at a fairly young age and was buried here. Also in the cemetery are graves of locals killed in the Ayr Carpet Works fire of 1876, and James MacNaughton of Smithfield, who constructed the railway from Newtyle to Dundee.

The Way descends steps to Craigholm Bridge. This footbridge was opened on 8 November 1974 by Provost Campbell Howie and gets its name from the two parts of Ayr that it links – Craigie and Holmston. Under the bridge is a large pool in the river, known as Craigie Weel.

Craigie House stands to the north of Craigholm Bridge. The house was erected around 1730 and it has been speculated that the architect responsible may have been John Smith. It is a rather fine Georgian building. The central block of the house, which is a typical Georgian building of three floors and a large projecting bay on the southern front. Advancing wings linked by curving corridors were added around 1770. Around 1837 a large Doric porch was added, perhaps the work of W. H. Playfair. Playfair also designed the Campbell of Craigie burial mausoleum in St Quivox kirkyard in 1822.

Craigie House was owned by the Wallace family, and it was erected to replace their older tower house of Newton Castle, which was located further west, but which was regarded as too uncomfortable for Georgian tastes, and in fact was partially destroyed in a storm of 1701. The new house was built outwith the town, on part of the estate, and the name was taken from the ancient seat of the Wallaces, Craigie Castle, the ruins of which can be seen to the east of Symington, near Craigie village.

The builder of the house, Sir Thomas Wallace, 5th Baronet of Craigie, was the last in the male line, and the estate passed to his daughter, who had married John Dunlop of that Ilk. In 1783 ownership of Craigie estate passed to William Campbell, who had made his fortune in India, and the Campbell family owned it for over 150 years until it was sold to Ayr Town Council in 1940 for £12,500.

After being purchased by the council, Craigie House was requisitioned for army use, after which it was used as a hotel for a time. It latterly became part of Craigie College of Education, a teacher training seminary, which was established in 1964. This is now part of Paisley University, and forms their Ayr campus.

From Craigholm Bridge the Way follows the right bank westwards through ornamental parkland, part of the Craigie grounds. There are attractive gardens, with roses and arbours. There are plenty of summer seats on which one can rest. To the south one can see the flats of Mill Brae Court. These were erected in 1999-2000 on the site of Ayr County hospital, which had stood here since 1881.

Behind some trees is the Ayrshire Archives centre, which can be visited, home to some of the old records associated with the county. West of this is the Dam Park sports arena, created in 1960. It has a running track, football field and athletics facilities, all overlooked by a grandstand.

The Way then passes the modern wing of Ayr College, erected in 1999 to plans of Boswell, Mitchell & Johnson. The large steel and stone structure dwarfs the original college building, further to the north, erected in 1966 to plans by Charles Toner.

Soon one sees two curving weirs, originally directing water into the Nether Mill of Ayr, which at one time was located on the south side of the river, where the car park now is. The weirs were rebuilt in 1816 of ashlar freestone. The Nether Mill was another ancient Ayr mill, the earliest reference to which dates from 1 October 1531, when a charter of feu was granted. There were two millwheels, one of which produced twenty horsepower, the other fifteen horsepower. Despite the head of water being only five feet, the mill had five pairs of stones. In 1794 a barley mill was added and in the following year a mill for the manufacture of snuff was created. During the Meal Riots of 1816 colliers from Newton upon Ayr attacked the mill and stole as much flour and meal as they could. In addition to this they destroyed the mill as far as possible, and on returning to Newton continued rioting by attacking shops in the burgh. The mills were demolished in 1941.

The Way keeps to the riverside, passing under Victoria Bridge, originally erected in 1898. The triple-span bridge was widened in 1961 and again in 1977 when the A79 road became part of a ring road around the centre of town. The piers in the water indicate the stages of building, the upper half of concrete, the lower of sandstone.

On the right is Ayr Fire Station, built in 1963 on the site of Content House to plans by J. & J. A. Carrick. Some of the old stone from the small mansion can be seen reused in the fire station building. Content was owned by the MacIlwraith family, who were prominent businessmen and ship-owners. Sir Thomas MacIlwraith (1835-1900) was three times Premier of Queensland in Australia.

Immediately west of the fire station the path goes under the Water Bridge, which carries the railway line. This is still used as part of the Glasgow to Stranraer line. Ayr station is located just to the south. The bridge was opened in 1856 when the line from Ayr was extended south towards Stranraer. It has four arches, each with a span of 60 feet. Previously Ayr Station was located in North Harbour Street. The station remains in use, an electrified line heading north to Glasgow. The line southwards is operated by diesel engines. A path can be followed back round to the right and up onto the 'Cagewalk', which is cantilevered out of the side of the railway bridge. This gives pedestrian access to the south side of the river and towards Ayr Station.

The way continues along the north side of the river, past the high flats of Riverside Place, erected 1968-70, to the northern end of Turner's Bridge. This is a cast iron foot bridge that was erected in 1900 by A. M. Turner, to allow his workers (most of whom lived on the north side of the river) to cross quickly to his Ayr and Newton Brewery, which was located on the south side of the river, where the flats of Blackfriars Court now stand. Looking south from here one can see the tall gothic Wallace Tower, erected in 1834 and containing a statue of the hero.

From Turner's Bridge the path is followed along the north side of the river, towards the Auld Bridge. Across the water can be seen the Auld Kirk Halls, with the copper roof, and the old kirkyard around Ayr's Auld Kirk, which occupies the site of the Franciscan Grey Friars Monastery, which was founded in 1472. The Auld Kirk of St John the Baptist is the parish church of Ayr. It was erected in 1654-6 when Cromwell's army took over the

Auld Kirk of St. John

ancient church of St John, which was located on the west side of
the town. To compensate the residents, Cromwell's government
paid one thousand merks towards the cost of erecting a new
church. This in fact cost £1733.

The Auld Kirk is a fairly plain and simple building,
constructed of rubble masonry. It is T-shaped in plan. There are
small lancet windows on the lower floor and larger gothic
windows on the gables. In 1836 the church was altered to plans by
David Bryce. The church is open to the public by arrangement on
Saturday mornings as part of Scotland's Churches Scheme. The
interior of the church is very fine, with much of interest to be
seen. There are Corinthian columns supporting the lofts, and the
pulpit is a double-decker version. Also within can be seen a
number of old relics, including the statue of Rev John Welsh
(1568-1622) that was formerly located in a garden off the High
Street, and a rare example of an 'Obit' board, recording donations
given to the poor. Here also is a model of the ship Arethusa.

The old kirkyard of Ayr has a number of interesting stones
within it. Visible from the path alongside the river is the headstone
erected in 1814 by the Incorporated Trades of Ayr to mark the
graves of seven Covenanting martyrs. There were originally eight

Covenanters held in Ayr tolbooth awaiting execution, but the hangman absconded to avoid having to carry out the deed. At length one of the Covenanters was allowed his freedom if he would agree to hang the other seven. Thus Cornelius Anderson succumbed and on 27 December 1666 he hanged his friends – James Smith, Alexander MacMillan, James MacMillan, John Short, George MacCartney, John Graham and John Muirhead. Anderson was then taken to Irvine where he had to hang two other Covenanters. He was then given a new life in Ireland, but died within a short time in a house fire, perhaps suicide.

The old lichgate that gives access to the kirkyard from the Kirkport and the High Street dates from 1656. On the wall is a plaque indicating the whereabouts of graves of a number of contemporaries of Robert Burns. These include Robert Aiken, Provost William Ferguson, Dr George Charles, John Ballantyne, Rev Dr William MacGill and David MacWhinnie.

Hanging on the walls of the lichgate are two iron mortsafes, one dated 1816. These were used in the early nineteenth century when body snatching was rife. To prevent fresh bodies being dug up and taken to the universities of Glasgow and Edinburgh for dissection, these mortsafes were clamped around the coffin which was then placed in the ground. The weight of the safe meant that it was too heavy for body snatchers to lift under the cover of darkness. After a few weeks, once the body had decayed

Ayr Martyrs' Grave

Auld Bridge, Ayr

sufficiently to be of no use to the dissectionist, the grave was reopened and the mortsafe removed, ready for the next coffin.

On the wall of the kirk is a monument to Rev William Adair, its first minister. Other interesting graves in the kirkyard include that to John Smith, 'the father of Scottish botany'.

The path continues to Riverside Place, at the Auld Bridge. To the south can be seen the back of the large stores of the High Street along the riverside. The first main block is of Bhs, built in 1984 but incorporating facades of 1883 on the High Street. Following on is Marks and Spencer, and here the path is cantilevered over the river. Marks and Spencer was erected in 1974.

At the River Cottage Restaurant the Way turns left to cross the Auld Bridge, the oldest surviving bridge across the River Ayr. The bridge was probably erected in the fifteenth century (it is mentioned in the Burgh Charters of 1440) although some claim that it is much older. In 1491 King James IV had to cross the river and he gifted ten shillings which was to be given to the masons who were at that time either building the new bridge, or perhaps repairing the old one.

On the parapet of the Auld Bridge is an old sundial, though unfortunately the gnomon has been broken. At the north end of the bridge can be seen the remains of old buildings, with a fireplace and windows visible. A plaque indicates that this was the site of the Bridge Port, a gate that prevented access to the burgh of Ayr at times. To the north of the River Ayr was a separate town, Newton upon Ayr, joined later by the planned town of Wallacetown.

At the north end of the Auld Bridge is the Black Bull Hotel, known in Burns' day as Simpson's Inn. It was here that Burns' father met John Murdoch. The inn is located in River Street, and along the front of it are some traditional buildings. Here also is the former River Street Mission Hall, erected in 1878 and now the Bridge Project. There are public toilets, inns and cafes in River Street.

On the walls of the Auld Bridge can be seen a couple of bronze plaques. One of these commemorates Robert Burns, who wrote his famous poem, 'The Brigs of Ayr', in the autumn of 1786 whilst the New Bridge was being erected. Burns' poem relates how the two bridges begin talking to each other about their relative merits. In it the Auld Brig predicts that it will 'be a brig

New Bridge, Ayr

when ye're a shapeless cairn', a prophecy that was to come true, for the New Bridge of 1786-8 was weak in design and suffered in a flood in 1877, after which it had to be demolished.

The second plaque commemorates the renovation of the Auld Bridge between 1907-10. At that time the bridge was dangerous and decaying and there was a proposal that it should be demolished. However, there was an outcry against this, mainly due to the bridge's association with Robert Burns, and a campaign to have it restored commenced. This was successful, so the bridge was closed and rebuilt.

Walkers making their way from the Auld Bridge to the New Bridge need to leave the river side for a spell. Auld Bridge Street, which is little more than a cobbled lane, leads south from the bridge to the High Street, Ayr's main shopping centre. Auld Bridge Street meets the High Street at an attractive open part of the street known as the Fish Cross. Here are numerous shops, inns and cafes, with all form of services required by a large town.

One has to walk down the High Street, which is partially pedestrianised, to its end at New Bridge Street and Sandgate. On the southern corner stands Ayr Town Hall, a massive classical building with a spire 217 feet in height, visible for miles around. The original building was erected in 1827-32 to plans by Thomas Hamilton but was extended along High Street in 1878-81 by

Loudoun Hall

Campbell Douglas & Sellars.

In the roadway at the T-junction some large granite stones can be noticed, marking the site of Ayr's ancient market cross. The Malt Cross, as it was known, was probably erected in 1697 to replace a timber cross. Tradition claims that Maggie Osborne was executed here for witchcraft. The cross was removed in 1778 in readiness for the opening up of New Bridge Street.

Walkers keeping to the Way should use the pedestrian crossing to cross New Bridge Street, then pass through the Boat Vennel and into South Harbour Street. At the start of Boat Vennel is a bronze model of Loudoun Hall, Ayr's oldest house, which still stands in the vennel. The house was erected in 1513 by merchant James Tait, but it was purchased by Sir Hew Campbell of Loudoun in 1539 as his town house. The Campbells of Loudoun were hereditary sheriffs of Ayrshire, and it was from this family that it gained its present name. Mary Queen of Scots is claimed to have slept here in August 1563. The hall latterly declined into slums and was in danger of being demolished. It was saved by the 4th Marquis of Bute in 1937 and it was subsequently restored in 1952 to plans by Robert Hurd. It was then presented to the people of Ayr. Today it forms a community hall, and it is often open to the public for exhibitions and during the summer months. Within the open area at the Hall is a carved seat, made from stone, wood and iron. A carving in the wall states 'I byde my time', which is the Campbell of Loudoun motto. At the west end of the Boat Vennel can be seen a steel rudder and chain from a ship.

An alternative route is to keep to the north side of the river between the two bridges, following River Street westwards from the Auld Bridge. The New Bridge leads onto Newton's Main Street. Here is the Carnegie Library, Ayr's main library which has a local history library on the first floor and a large reference section on the ground floor, in addition to a general lending collection.

The New Bridge as it stands dates from 1877-79, and was designed by the engineers Blyth and Cunningham. It cost £15,000 to build, the five arches and piers constructed of sandstone, the parapets of white granite. It stands on the site of the earlier New Bridge, already mentioned, erected to designs that are believed to have been drawn up by Robert Adam. Certainly Ayr Town Council paid 'Mr Adams of London' for plans, but the local architect, Alexander Stevens, is thought to have overseen the work, and may have made alterations to the design. In any case, the bridge was erected at a cost of £4000 and opened to great aplomb, only for it to be damaged when a storm caused the River Ayr to flood and batter against it, causing irreparable destruction.

South Harbour Street forms the last stretch of the River Ayr Way. Along the first stretch of the street are traditional buildings with a variety of inns (Steamboat Tavern and Ye Olde Forte Bar), restaurants and fast food outlets. Walkers should follow the street along the south side of the harbour, past the Waterside Restaurant, which was originally erected as a lifeboat station but which was closed in 1932. Behind it are some large cylindrical masonry piers in the river, at one time carrying a steel-frame railway bridge. This had been erected in 1899 to bring trains to the south side of the harbour, but it was closed and removed in 1978.

On the south side of the street can be seen a small open turret on top of a sloping masonry wall. This is known locally as Miller's Folly, for the turret was erected around 1870 by John Miller (1820-1910), who had purchased the former Cromwell barracks site in Ayr and began to feu off the ground for housing. He converted the former tower of St John's Church into a home for himself, known as Fort Castle, in which he collected numerous antiquities. Miller was originally employed as a gunsmith, and he claimed to be a Baron as a result of his ownership of the citadel, which had in 1663 been created into the Barony of Montgomerieston for the Earl of Eglinton.

The sloping walls, however, are much older, and form part of the Cromwellian citadel that was erected here in 1652. This was one of five forts established by the Protectorate in Scotland. As already mentioned, the Church of St John was taken over, and the tower was converted into a lookout tower. At one time 1,200 soldiers were billeted here. The fort remained in use for only eight years before being given to the Earl of Eglinton, in recompense for his losses during the time of the Protectorate.

At the northern end of the fort is a replica cannon. This is based on a cast iron saker and carriage. The nine feet long barrel could fire six pound cast iron balls. The cannon weighs 1240 pounds and required between three and six men to operate it.

Across the road from Miller's Folly and the fort is the Citadel Leisure Centre, originally Ayr Baths (erected in 1970-2) but which was extended to include other facilities and reopened in August 1997 as the Citadel. Here starts an exercise route known as the 'Lang Scots Mile'. A Scots mile was 1984 yards in length, which was longer than an English mile of 1760 yards. A brisk walk along this route is reckoned to burn between 110 and 190 calories.

On the quayside are blocks of flats, each of which has been named in honour of former soldiers, for where Ayr Baths was built had been the site of Ayr Barracks. Here was the headquarters of the Royal Scots Fusiliers, later Royal Highland Fusiliers, and war memorials to this regiment can be seen at the west end of the County Buildings, overlooking Place de Saint-Germain-en-Laye, and in Burns Statue Square. One of the blocks is named Donnini Court after Dennis Donnini (1925-45), who was awarded the Victoria Cross posthumously.

The south side of Ayr Harbour is now much quieter than it once was, though sometimes ships and pleasure boats tie up here. There are also jetties for yachts, and during the summer season the last sea-going paddle steamer in the world, the *P.S. Waverley,* makes Ayr one of its ports of call. The vessel was built in 1946 by A. & J. Inglis, to replace a steamer of the same name, sunk off Dunkirk by enemy action in 1940. From here trips around Arran or the Kyles of Bute can be taken.

The Way can be followed along a path to the start of the esplanade. It then strikes north to the top end of the former shipyard slip. This dock was created in 1881 and ships as large as 1,597 tons were built here. The yard went into decline and the last ship built was in 1929. The yard latterly was only used for repairs. It is now abandoned and modern flats erected to the east. At the head of the dock is a former fishing boat, the *Watchful,* launched in 1959 and based at the Maidens for a time, perched on a concrete cradle. This was placed here in 1995 to commemorate the centuries of fishing that was carried on from this harbour and in memory of those who lost their lives at sea.

Around the docks are a number of interesting carvings and sculptures, all recollecting the nautical and shipbuilding themes. Among these are lengths of chain on end, an old swage block, hooks and the map reference 55°28'.00N, 04°38'.00W, indicative of Ayr harbour. On the brick wall of the former shipyard are studs outlining a boat's sheer plan. A steel footbridge across the slip dock accesses Churchill Tower where there is a small general store and a plaque giving information on three of those soldiers commemorated by the names of the flats.

At the northern end of the dock the walker turns onto the South Pier. This guards the mouth of the harbour and extends about 600 yards into the bay. At the western end is a small lighthouse. To the south of the lighthouse St Nicholas Rock can be seen, a natural outcrop that is covered at high tide. The end of the pier marks the west end of the River Ayr Way, around forty miles or so from Glenbuck Loch.

The northern harbour has to be accessed from the New Bridge. The former Darlington Place Church, erected in 1860, is now the base for the Borderline Theatre Company. New buildings extend along the street west from here, occupying the site of Ayr

Goods Station, originally opened on 11 August 1840 as Ayr Station. North Harbour Street continues as far as the entrance to Ayr Docks, still used for transporting coal, iron and spirits. Within the dock area is Ayr Lighthouse, erected in 1841-3 to plans by Robert Paton. It is located in a rather inland position, but when aligned with the leading lights on the harbour piers gives positioning to approaching ships.

Ayr Dock is located beyond. This was created in 1878 by carving out a basin from the solid rock. Today the dock is operated by Associated British Ports. Access around this northern part of the harbour is limited, and there is little of any historical interest to be seen.

MAP 1 - *Glenbuck to Wellwood*

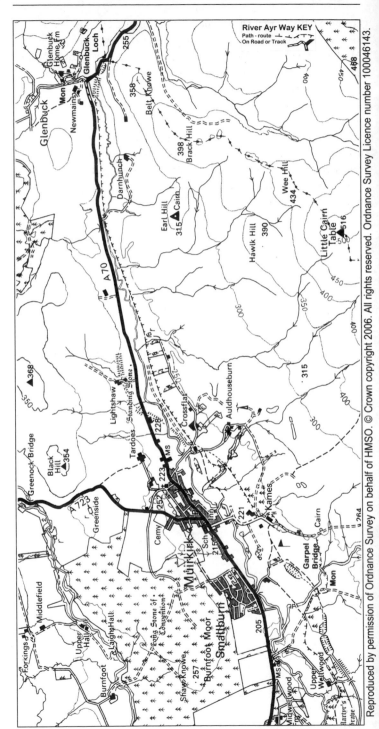

Map 2 - *Wellwood to Daldilling*

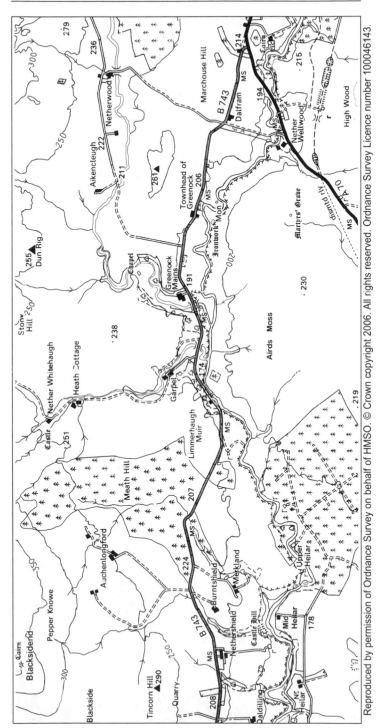

MAP 3 - *Daldilling to the Haugh*

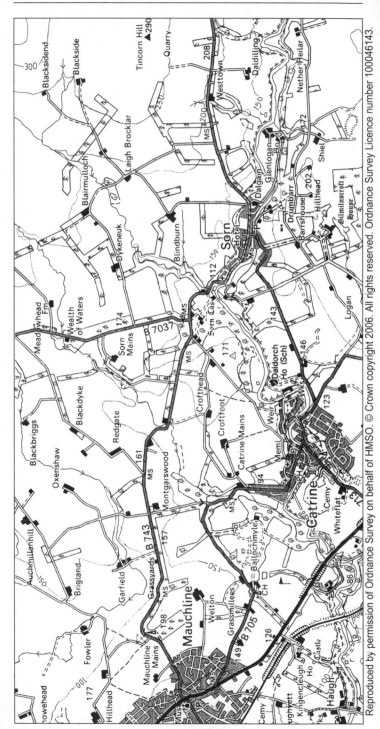

MAP 4 - *The Haugh to Gadgirth Bridge*

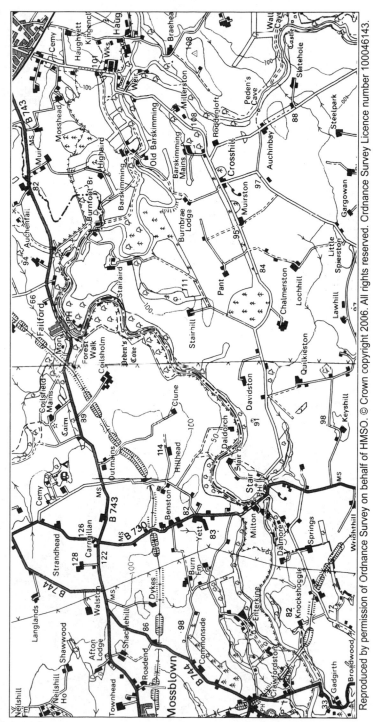

MAP 5 - *Gadgirth Bridge to Ayr*

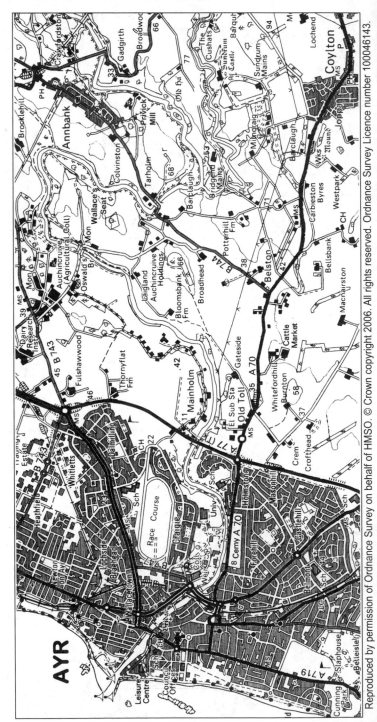

Bibliography

Baird, John G. A., *Muirkirk in Bygone Days*, W. S. Smith, Muirkirk, 1910.

Barber, Derek, *Steps through Stair*, Stair Parish Church, Stair, 2000.

Boyle, Andrew M., *The Ayrshire Book of Burns-Lore*, Alloway Publishing, Darvel, 1985.

Close, Rob, *Ayrshire & Arran: an Illustrated Architectural Guide*, RIAS, Edinburgh 1992.

Dalziel, Robert, & Harrison, Terry, *200 Years of Catrine and Sorn Parish: A Cotton Tale,* Countryside, Brinscall, 1987.

Davis, Michael C., *The Castles and Mansion of Ayrshire*, Davis, Ardrishaig, 1991.

Dyer, William F., *My Memoirs of a Mansion fit for a Lady but not for Me,* W. F. Dyer, Livingston, 2003.

Faulds, Rev. M. H. & Tweedie, William, *The Cherrypickers*, Cumnock & Doon Valley District Council, Lugar, 1981.

Findlay, Thomas, *Garan 1631 to Muirkirk 1950*, Findlay, Muirkirk, 1980.

Martin, David J., *Auchincruive,* Scottish Agricultural College, Edinburgh, 1994.

Morris, James A., *The Brig of Ayr and Something of its Story*, Stephen & Pollock, Ayr, 1910.

Pettigrew, David, *Old Muirkirk and Glenbuck*, Stenlake, Cumnock, 1996.

Rab the Rambler, *Rambles on the Banks of the Ayr*, Ayrshire Post, Ayr, 1884.

Reid, Denholm T., *Old Annbank and Mossblown*, Stenlake, Catrine, 2005.

Thomson, Rev J. H., *The Martyr Graves of Scotland*, Oliphant, Anderson & Ferrier, Edinburgh, n.d.

Tucker, D. Gordon, *Ayrshire Hone-Stones*, AANHS, Ayr, 1983.

Wilson, James Pearson, *The Last Miller,* AANHS, Ayr, 2000.

Wilson, Rhona, *Old Catrine and Sorn*, Stenlake, Cumnock, 1997.

Index

Page numbers in italics refer to illustrations